Data Science for Supply Chain Forecast

Nicolas Vandeput

1st edition – 2018
nicolas.vandeput@supchains.com

Contents

Data Science for Supply Chain Forecast   vii

I   Statistical Forecast   1

1. Moving Average   3
2. Forecast Error   15
3. Exponential Smoothing   27
4. Underfitting   37
5. Double Exponential Smoothing   41
6. Model Optimization   53
7. Double Smoothing with Damped Trend   61
8. Overfitting   67
9. Triple Exponential Smoothing   71
10. Outliers   87
11. Triple Additive Exponential smoothing   99

II Machine Learning   109

12 Machine Learning   111

13 Tree   121

14 Parameter Optimization   127

15 Forest   135

16 Feature Importance   143

17 Extremely Randomized Trees 147

18 Feature Optimization   153

19 Adaptive Boosting   167

20 Exogenous Information & Leading Indicators   177

21 Extreme Gradient Boosting   187

22 Categories   197

23 Clustering   205

Glossary   221

Preface

Tomorrow's supply chain is expected to provide many improved benefits for all stakeholders, and this across much more complex and interconnected networks than the current supply chain.

Today, the practice of supply chain science is striving for excellence: innovative and integrated solutions are based on new ideas, new perspectives and new collaborations, thus enhancing the power offered by data science.

This opens up tremendous opportunities to design new strategies, tactics and operations to achieve greater anticipation, a better final customer experience and an overall enhanced supply chain.

As supply chain generally account between 60% and 90% of all company costs (excluding financial services), any drive toward excellence will undoubtedly be equally impactful on a company's performance as well as on its final consumer satisfaction.

This book, written by Nicolas Vandeput, is a carefully developed work emphasizing how and where data science (with its systems integration and knowledge) can effectively lift the supply chain process higher up the excellence ladder.

This is a gap-bridging book from both the research and the practitioner's perspective, it is a great source of information and value.

Firmly grounded in scientific research principles, this book deploys a comprehensive set of approaches particularly useful in tackling the critical challenges that practitioners and researchers face in today and tomorrow's (supply chain) business environment.

Prof. Dr. Ir. Alassane B. NDIAYE
Professor of Logistics & Transport Systems
Universite Libre de Bruxelles, Belgium

Data Science for Supply Chain Forecast

Artificial intelligence is the new electricity
Andrew Ng[1]

In the same way electricity revolutionized the second half of the XIXth century, allowing industries to produce more with less, AI will drastically impact the following decades. While some companies already use this new electricity to cast new light upon their business, others are definitely still using old oil lamps; or even candles, using manpower to manually change these candles every hour of the day in order to keep the business running.

As you will discover in this book, artificial intelligence (AI) & machine learning (ML) are not just a question of coding skills. Using data science to solve a problem will require a scientific mindset more than coding skills. We will discuss many different models and algorithms in the latter chapters. But as you will see, you do not need to be an IT wizard to apply these models. There is another more important story behind these: a story of experimentations, observation and questioning everything; a true scientific method applied to supply chain. In the field of data science as well as for supply chain, simple questions do not come with simple answers. To answer these questions, you will need to both be a scientist and use the right tools. In this book, we will discuss both.

Supply Chain Forecast Within all supply chains lies the question of planning. The better we evaluate the future, the better we can prepare ourselves. The question of future uncertainty, how to reduce it or how to protect yourself against this unknown has always been crucial for every supply chain. From negotiating contract volumes with suppliers to setting safety stock targets, everything relates to the ultimate question:

---
[1]Andrew Ng is the co-founder of Coursera the leading online-classes platform

What is tomorrow going to be like?

Yesterday, big companies provided forecast softwares that allowed businesses to use a statistical forecast as the backbone of their S&OP[1] process. These statistical forecast models were proposed 60 years ago by Holt & Winters[2] and didn't change much in the last 50 years: at the core of any statistical forecast tool, you still find exponential smoothing. Software companies sell the idea that they can add a bit of extra intelligence into it, or some less-known statistical model, but in the end it all goes back to exponential smoothing, which we will discuss in the first part of this book. Yesterday, one analyst on his own personal computer couldn't compete with these models.

Today, things have changed. Thanks to the increase in computing power, the in-flow of data and the availability of free tools, one can make a difference. **You** can make a difference. With a bit of coding skills and an appetite for experimentation, powered by machine learning models, you will be able to bring to any business more value than any off-the-shelf forecast software can deliver.

We often hear that the recent rise of artificial intelligence (or machine learning) is due to an increasing amount of data available as well as cheaper computing power. This is not entirely true. Two other effects explain the recent interest in machine learning. In the previous years, many machine learning models were improved, giving better results. As these models were becoming better & faster, the tools to use them became more user-friendly. It is much easier today to use powerful machine learning models than it was 10 years ago.

Can I do this? Is this book for me? This book has been written for supply chain practitioners, forecasters and analysts who are looking to go the extra mile[3]. You do not need technical IT skills to start using the models of this book today. You do not need a dedicated server or expensive software licences: only your own computer. You do not need a PhD in mathematics: we will only use mathematics when they are directly useful to tweak and understand the models. More often than not — especially for machine learning — a deep understanding of the mathematical inner workings of a model will not be necessary to optimize it and understand its limitations.

---

[1] The sales and operations planning (S&OP) process focuses on aligning mid and long-term demand and supply.
[2] See page 32 for more information about Holt & Winters.
[3] Even though we will focus on supply chain demand forecast, the principles & models explained here can be applied to any forecast problem.

The Data Scientist's Mindset

As the business world discovers data science, many supply chain practitioners still rely on rules of thumbs and simple approximations to run their businesses. Most often, most of the work is done directly in Excel. A paradigm shift will be needed to go from manual approximations done in Excel towards automated powerful models in Python. We need to leave oil lamps behind and move to electricity. This is what we will do – step by step – in this book. Before discussing our supply chain data-scientist tools, let's discuss what our data scientist mindset should be.

Data is gold If artificial intelligence is the new electricity – allowing us to achieve more in a smarter way – data is the modern gold. Gold, unfortunately, does not grow on trees; it comes from gold ore that needs to be extracted and cleaned. Just like data: it needs to be mined, extracted and cleaned. We even have to think where to mine to get the data. As supply chain data scientists, we are both goldsmiths and miners. Even though this book does not cover the specific topic of data cleaning nor the question of data governance, it will show you how to magnify gold in jewelry. Always treat data as if it were gold ore: it is precious but needs to be cleaned and refined in order to become usable.

Start small, iterate It is easy to lose yourself in details as you try to model the real business world. To avoid this, we will always start tackling broad supply chain questions with simple models. And then, we will iterate on these models, adding complexity layers one by one. It is an illusion to think that one could grasp all the complexity of a supply chain at once in one model. As your understanding of a supply chains grows, so does the complexity of your model.

Experiment! There is no definitive answer nor model to each supply chain question. We are not in a world of one-size-fits-all. A model that worked for another company might not work for you. This book will propose you many models & ideas and will give you the tools to play with them and to experiment. Which one to choose in the end is up to you! I can only encourage you to experiment small variations on them – and then bigger ones! – until you find the one that suits your business.

Unfortunately, many people forget that experimenting means trial & error. Which means that you will face the risk of failing. Experimenting with new ideas and models is not a linear task: days or weeks can be invested in dead ends. On the other hand, a single stroke of genius can drastically improve a model. What is important is to fail fast and start a new cycle rapidly. Don't get discouraged by a couple of days without improvement.

Automation is the key to fast experimentation As you will see, we will need to run tens, hundreds or even thousands of experiments on some datasets to find the best model. In order to do so, only automation can help us out. It is tremendously important to keep our data workflow fully automated in order to be able to run these experiments without hurdle. Only automation will allow you to scale your work.

Automation is the key to reliability As your model will grow in complexity and your datasets in size, you will need to be able to reliably populate results (and act upon them). Only an automated data workflow together with an automated model will give you reliable results over and over again. Manual work will slow you down and create random mistakes, which will result *in fine* in frustration.

Don't get mislead by overfitting and luck As we will see in chapter 8, overfitting (i.e. your model will work extremely well on your current dataset but fail to perform well on new data) is the #1 curse for data scientists. Do not get fooled by luck or overfitting. You should always treat astonishing results with suspicion and ask yourself the question: *"Can I replicate these results on new unseen data?"*.

Sharing is caring Science needs openness. You will be able to create better models if you take the time to share their inner workings with your team. Openly sharing results (good and bad) will also create trust among the team. Many people are afraid to share bad results, but it is worth doing so. Sharing bad results will allow you to trigger a debate among your team to build a new and better model. Maybe someone external will bring a brand-new idea that will allow you to improve your model.

Simplicity over complexity As a model grows bigger, there is always a temptation to add more and more specific rules and exceptions. Do not go down this road. As more special rules add up in a model, the model will lose its ability to perform reliably well on new data. And soon, you will lose the understanding of all the different interdependences. You should always prefer a structural fix to a specific new rule (also known as *quick fix*). As the pile of quick fixes grows bigger, the potential amount of interdependences will exponentially increase and you will not be able to identify why your model works in a specific way.

Focus on the point As a last piece of advice, you should always focus on the point. Clarity comes from simplicity. When communicating your results, always ask yourself some questions:

Who am I communicating to?
What are they interested in?
Do I show them everything they are interested in?
Do I show them only what they are interested in?

In a world of big data, it is easy to drown someone in numbers and graphs. Just keep your communication simple and straight to the point. Remember that our brain easily analyzes and extrapolates graphs and curves. So prefer a simple graph to a table of data when communicating your results.

Perfection is achieved, not when there is nothing more to add, but when there is nothing left to take away.
Antoine de Saint-Exupery (1940-1944)

The Data Scientist's Tools

We will use two tools to build our models, experiment and share our results.

Excel Excel is the data analyst's Swiss knife. It will allow you to easily perform simple calculations and plot data. The big advantage of Excel compared to any programming language is that we can **see** the data. It is much easier to debug a model or to test a new one if you see how the data is transformed by each step of computation. Therefore, Excel can be a first go-to to experiment with new models or data.

Excel also has many limitations. It won't perform well on big datasets and will hardly allow you to automate difficult tasks.

Python Python is a programming language initially published in 1991 by Guido van Rossum, a Dutch computer scientist. If Excel is a Swiss knife, Python is a full army of construction machines awaiting instructions from any data scientist. Python will allow you to perform computations on huge datasets in an automated and fast way. Python also comes with many libraries dedicated to data analysis (`pandas`), scientific computations (`NumPy` & `SciPy`) or machine learning (`scikit-learn`). These will soon be your best friends.

Why Python? We chose to use Python over other programming languages as it is both user-friendly (it is easy to read & understand) and one of the most used programming languages in the world. In 2018, it was the programming language that was the most googled and it is the most commonly used for machine learning.

Should you start learning Python? Yes, you should.

Excel will be perfect to visualize results and the different data transformation steps you perform, but it won't allow you to scale your models to bigger datasets nor to easily automate any data cleaning. Excel is also unable to run any machine learning algorithm.

Many practitioners are afraid to learn a coding language. Everyone knows a colleague who uses some macros/VBA in Excel — maybe you are this colleague — and the complexity of these macros might be frightening to the profane. **Python is much simpler than Excel macros**. It is also **much more powerful**. As you will see by yourself in the following chapters, even the most advanced machine learning models won't require so many lines of code or complex functions. It means that you do not have to be an IT genius to use machine learning on your own computer. You can do it yourself, today. Python will give you a definitive edge compared to anyone using Excel. Today is a great day to start learning Python. Many resources are available: videos, blogs, articles, books... You can, for example, look for Python courses on the following online platforms:

> www.edx.org
> www.coursera.org
> www.udemy.com
> www.datacamp.com

I do personally recommend the MIT class *"Introduction to Computer Science and Programming Using Python"* available on EdX [8]. This will teach you everything you need to know about Python to start using the models presented in this book.

We will also briefly introduce the most useful concepts in chapter 1 to help you out with the first code extracts.

How to Read This Book

Data Science for Supply Chain Forecast is written the way I wish someone had explained me how to forecast supply chain products some years ago. It

How to Read This Book

is divided into two parts: we will first discuss old-school statistical models and then move to machine learning models.

Old-school statistics and Machine Learning One could think that these statistical models are already outdated and useless as machine learning models will take over. But this is wrong. These old-school models will allow us to *understand* and *see* the demand patterns in our supply chain. Machine learning models, unfortunately, won't provide us any explanation nor understanding of the different patterns. Machine learning is only focused on one thing: getting the right answer. The *how* does not matter. This is why both the statistical models and the machine learning models will be helpful for you.

Concepts & Models The book is divided into many chapters: each of them is either a new model or a new concept. This will allow us to build our understanding of the field of data science & forecast step by step. Each new model or concept will allow to overcome a limitation or to go one step further in terms of forecast accuracy.
On the other hand, obviously, not all forecast models are explained here. We will focus on the models that have proven their value in the world of supply chain forecast.

Do It Yourself We also take the decision not to use any prebuilt forecast function from Python or Excel. The objective of this book is not to teach you how to use a software. It is twofold. First, it is for you to be able to experiment with different models on your own datasets. This means that you will have to tweak the models and experiment with different variations. You will only be able to do this if you take the time to implement these models yourself. Second, it is for you to acquire an in-depth knowledge on how the different models work as well as their strengths and limitations. Implementing the different models yourself will allow you to learn by doing as you test them along the way.
At the end of each chapter, you will find a *Do-It-Yourself* section that will show you a step-by-step implementation of the different models. I can only advise you to start testing these models on your own datasets ASAP.

Other resources

You can download the Python codes shown in this book as well as the Excel templates on www.supchains.com/book-ressources (password: SupChains).

There is also a glossary at the end of the book where you can find a short description of all the specific terms we will use. Do not hesitate to consult it if you are unsure about a term or acronym.

Part I

Statistical Forecast

Chapter 1

Moving Average

The first forecast model we will develop is the simplest. As supply chain data scientists, we love to start experimenting quickly. First, with a simple model, then with more complex ones.

Idea

The moving average model is based on the idea that future demand is similar to the recent demand we observed. With this model, we will simply assume that the forecast is the average of the demand during the last *n* periods. If you look at demand on a monthly basis, this could translate as *"We predict the demand in June to be the average of March, April and May"*.

Model

If we formalize this idea, we obtain this formula:

$$f_t = \frac{1}{n} \sum_{i=1}^{n} d_{t-i}$$

Where,

> *n* is the number of periods we take the average of;
> d_t is the demand we observed during period *t*;
> f_t is the forecast we made for period *t*.

Initialization As you will see for further models, we always need to discuss how to initialize the forecast for the first periods. For the moving average method, we won't have a forecast until we have enough historical demand observations. So the first forecast will be done for $t = n+1$.

Future forecast Once we are out of the historical period, we simply define any future forecast as the last one that was done based on historical demand. That means that with this model, the future forecast is flat. This will be one of the major restrictions of this model: its inability to extrapolate any trend.

Notations

In the scientific literature, you will often see the output you want to predict noted as y. It is due to the mathematical convention where we want to estimate y based on x. A prediction (a forecast in our case) would then be noted $\hat{y}$. This hat represents the idea that we do an estimation of y. In order to make our models and equations as simple to read and understand as possible, we will avoid this usual convention and use something more practical:

Demand will be noted as **d**

Forecast will be noted as **f**

When we want to point to a specific occurrence of the forecast (or the demand) at time t, we will note it f_t (or d_t). Typically,

d_0 is the demand at period 0 (e.g. first month, first day, etc.).

f_0 is the forecast for the demand of period 0.

We will call the demand of each period, a **demand observation**. For example, if we measure our demand on monthly buckets, that means we will have 12 demand observations per year.

Insights

On figure 1.1, we have plotted two different moving average forecasts.

As you can see, the moving average forecast where $n = 1$ is a rather specific case: the forecast is the demand with a one-period lag. This is what we call a **naïve forecast**: "tomorrow will be just as today". A naïve

Do It Yourself

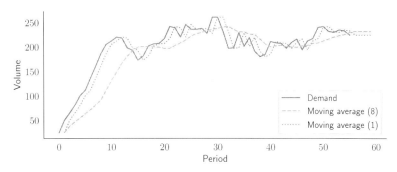

Figure 1.1: Moving average

forecast is interesting as it will react fast to a changing demand, but on the other hand it will also be sensitive to **noise** and outliers.

> **Noise** In statistics, the noise is an unexplained variation in the data. It is often due to the randomness of the different processes at hand.

To decrease this sensitivity, we can go for a moving average based on more previous demand observations ($n > 1$). Unfortunately, the model will also take more time to react to a changing demand level. On figure 1.1 you can observe that the moving average with $n = 8$ takes more time to adapt to the changing demand level during the first phase. But during the second phase the forecast is more stable than the naïve one. **We have to make a trade-off between reactivity and smoothness**. As you will see, we will have to make this trade-off over and over again for all the exponential smoothing models that we will see later.

Do It Yourself

Excel

Let's build an example with a moving average model based on the last 3 demand occurrences ($n = 3$).

1. We start our data table by creating three columns:

    Date on column A
    Demand on column B
    Forecast on column C

    You can define the first line as Date = 1 (cell A2 = 1) and increase the date by one on each line.

2. For the sake of the example, we will always use the same dummy demand in Excel. You can type these numbers (starting on date 1 until date 10): 37, 60, 85, 112, 132, 145, 179, 198, 212, 232.
3. We can now define the first forecast on date 4. You can simply use the formula C5=AVERAGE(B2:B4) and copy-paste it until the end of the table. You can go until row 12 (date 11), which will be the last forecast based on historical demand.
4. As of then, the future forecasts will all be equivalent to this last point. You can use C13=C12 and copy-paste this formula until as far as you want to have a forecast. In the example, we go until date 13.
5. You should now have a table that looks like figure 1.2.

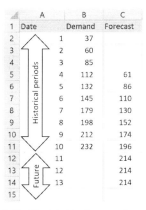

Figure 1.2: Final table for moving average

Python

If you are already familiar with Python and know that pandas are not just cute animals, you can skip this and jump to **Moving average function** on page 12.

If this is your first time with Python, let's take some time to quickly discuss and introduce the different libraries and data types we are going to use. Of course, the objective of this book is not to give you a full training about Python; if you wish an in-depth introduction (or if you are not yet convinced to use Python) please refer to the recommended courses on page xii.

Do It Yourself

How to install Python?

There are multiple ways to install Python on your computer. An easy way to do this is to install the anaconda distribution on www.anaconda.com/download. Anaconda is a well-known platform used by data scientists all over the world. It works on Windows, Mac & Linux. Anaconda will take care of installing all the Python libraries you need to run the different models that we are going to discuss and it will also install Spyder and Jupyter Notebook, two Python-code editors that you can use to type and run your code. Feel free to check both and use your favorite.

Lists

The most basic object we will use in Python is a `list`. In Python, a `list` is simply an ordered sequence of any number of objects (e.g. strings, numbers, other lists, more complex objects...). You can create a list by encoding these objects between []. Typically, we can define our first time series `ts` as this

```
ts = [1,2,3,4,5,6]
```

These `lists` are very efficient to store and manipulate objects, but are not meant for number computation. For example, if we want to add two different time series, we can't simply ask `ts + ts2`, as this is what we would get:

```
ts = [1,2,3,4,5,6]
ts2 = [10,20,30,40,50,60]
ts + ts2
Out: [1, 2, 3, 4, 5, 6, 10, 20, 30, 40, 50, 60]
```

Python is giving us back a new longer `list`. That's not exactly what we wanted.

Numpy

This is where the famous **NumPy**[1] library comes to help. Since its initial release in 2005, NumPy has offered us a new data type: a NumPy **array**. This is similar to a `list`, as it contains a sequence of different numeric values, but differs in that we can easily call any mathematical function on them. You can create one directly from a `list` like this:

---

[1] NumPy for Numeric Python. *Do they dream of numeric sheep?*

```
import numpy as np
ts = np.array([1,2,3,4,5,6])
```

As you will see, NumPy is most often imported as np. We can now simply add our array ts to any other array.

```
ts2 = np.array([10,20,30,40,50,60])
ts + ts2
Out: array([11, 22, 33, 44, 55, 66])
```

Note that the result is another NumPy array (and not a simple list). NumPy most often works very well directly with regular lists as we can use most of the NumPy functions directly on them. Here is an example:

```
alist = [1,2,3]
np.mean(alist)
Out: 2.0
```

You can always look for help on the NumPy official website[1] and, as you will see by yourself, most of your Google searches about NumPy functions will actually end up directly on their documentation.

Slicing

To select a particular value in a list (or an array), you simply have to indicate between [] the index of its location inside the list (array). The catch – as with many coding languages – is that the index starts at 0 and not at 1; so that the first element in your list will have the index 0, the second element the index 1, and so on.

```
alist = ["cat","dog","mouse"]
alist[1]
Out: "dog"
anarray = np.array([1,2,3])
anarray[0]
Out: 1
```

If you want to select multiple items at once, you can simply indicate a range of index with this format: start:end. If you do not give a start value, Python will assume it is 0. If you do not give an end, it will assume

---

[1] www.docs.scipy.org/doc/numpy/

Do It Yourself

the end of the list. Pay attention that the result will include the start element but exclude the end element.

```
alist = ["cat","dog","mouse"]
alist[1:]
Out: ["dog","mouse"]
anarray = np.array([1,2,3])
anarray[:1]
Out: np.array([1])
```

If you give a negative value as the end, Python will start counting backward from the last element of your list/array.

```
alist = ["cat","dog","mouse"]
alist[-1]
Out: ["mouse"]
alist[:-1]
Out: ["cat","dog"]
```

Pandas

Pandas is one of the most used libraries in Python (created by Wes McKinney in 2008). The name comes from... **pan**el **da**ta, as it helps to order data into tables. Think Excel-meet-databases in Python. This library introduces a new data type: a `DataFrame`. If you're a database person, just think about a `DataFrame` as an SQL table. If you're an Excel person, just imagine a `DataFrame` as an Excel table. Actually, a `DataFrame` is a sort of data table where each column would be a `NumPy array` with a specific name. That will be pretty handy as we can select each column of our `DataFrame` by its name.

There are many ways to create a `DataFrame`, let's create our first one by using a `list` of our two time series.

```
import pandas as pd
pd.DataFrame([ts,ts2])
```

```
Out:
     0   1   2   3   4   5
0    1   2   3   4   5   6
1   10  20  30  40  50  60
```

The convention is to import pandas as pd and to call the DataFrame df. The output we get is a DataFrame where we have 6 columns (named "0","1","2","3","4" and "5") and 2 rows (actually, they do also have a name – or index – "0" and "1").

We can easily edit the column names:

```
import pandas as pd
df = pd.DataFrame([ts,ts2])
df.columns = ["Day1","Day2","Day3","Day4","Day5","Day6"]
print(df)
```

```
Out:
    Day1  Day2  Day3  Day4  Day5  Day6
0      1     2     3     4     5     6
1     10    20    30    40    50    60
```

Pandas comes with a very simple and helpful official documentation[1]. When in doubt, do not hesitate a second to look into it. Just as for Numpy, most of your Google searches will end up there.

Slicing DataFrames You have many different techniques to slice a DataFrame to get the element or the part you want. This might be confusing for beginners, but you'll soon understand that each of these has its uses and advantages. Do not worry if you get confused or overwhelmed: you won't need to apply all of these right now.

- You can select a specific column by passing the name of this column directly to the DataFrame either with df["myColumn"] or even more directly with df.myColumn.
- You can select a row based on its index value by simply typing df[myIndexValue].
- If you want to select an element based on both its row and column, you can call the method .loc on the DataFrame and give it the index and the column you want. You can for example type df.loc[myIndexValue,"myColumn"]
- You can also use the same slicing method as for lists and arrays based on the position of the element you want to select. You then need to call the method .iloc to the DataFrame. Typically, to select the first element (top left corner), you can do df.iloc[0,0].

---

[1] www.pandas.pydata.org/pandas-docs/stable/

Do It Yourself

As a recap, here are all the techniques you can use to select a column and/or a row:

```
df["myColumn"]
df.myColumn
df[myIndexValue]
df.loc[myIndexValue,"myColumn"]
df.iloc[0,0]
```

Typically, in our following models, we will create a `DataFrame` to store our historical demand (column `Demand`) and our forecast (column `Forecast`). You can thus select only the forecast by simply typing `df.Forecast`.

Dictionaries

Another way to create a `DataFrame` is to construct it based on a `dictionary` of `lists` or `arrays`. A dictionary is a sort of list where each element has a unique name (and can be called by its name). You can create one by including between `{}` a `key` and a `value`, where the key must be a string (that's the unique name we were talking about) and the value can be anything.

```
dic = {"Small product":ts,"Big product":ts2}
dic
Out:
{'Small product': array([1, 2, 3, 4, 5, 6]),
 'Big product': array([10, 20, 30, 40, 50, 60])}
```

Here the `key` "Small product" will give you the value `ts`, whereas the key "Big product" will give you ts2.

```
dic["Small product"]
Out: array([1, 2, 3, 4, 5, 6])
dic["Small product"] + dic["Big product"]
Out: array([11, 22, 33, 44, 55, 66])
```

What is handy is that we can now create a DataFrame directly from this dictionary.

```
df = pd.DataFrame.from_dict(dic)
Out:
    Small product    Big product
0                1             10
1                2             20
```

6	2	3	30
7	3	4	40
8	4	5	50
9	5	6	60

We now have a DataFrame where each product has its own column and each row is another period.

Moving average function

Now that we have introduced pandas and NumPy, we can work on our very first forecast model. We will define a function moving_average that takes three inputs:

> **d:** a time series that contains the historical demand;
>
> **extra_periods:** the number of periods we want to forecast in the future;
>
> **n:** the number of periods we will average.

```python
def moving_average(d,extra_periods=1,n=3):

    # Transform the input into a numpy array
    d = np.array(d)
    # Historical period length
    cols = len(d)
    # Append np.nan into the demand array to cover future periods
    d = np.append(d,[np.nan]*extra_periods)
    # Define the forecast array
    f = np.full(cols+extra_periods,np.nan)

    # Create all the t+1 forecasts until end of historical period
    for t in range(n,cols+1):
        f[t] = np.mean(d[t-n:t])

    # Forecast for all extra periods
    f[cols+1:] = f[t]

    # Return a dataframe with the demand, forecast & error
    df = pd.DataFrame.from_dict({"Demand":d,"Forecast":f,"Error":d-f})

    return df
```

Do It Yourself

We have introduced two new elements in our code:

np.nan is a way to represent something that is not a number[1].
In our function, we used np.nan to store in f an initial dummy value that is not a number, before it gets replaced by actual values. If we had initialized f with actual digits (e.g. ones or zeroes), this could have been misleading in the future as we wouldn't know if these ones or zeroes where actual forecast values or just the dummy initial ones.

np.full(shape,value) this function will return an array of a certain shape, filled in with the given value.
In our function, we used np.full() to create the NumPy array of our forecast (f).

Note also that the input d (the historical demand) is transformed into a NumPy array to make sure that the function works even if d is passed as a pandas DataFrame or a simple list.

Our function moving_average(d,extra_periods,n) will return a DataFrame. We can save it for later use, as shown below with a dummy demand time series. Here is an example on how to use it to forecast a dummy demand time series:

```
import pandas as pd
import numpy as np

d =[28,19,18,13,19,16,19,18,13,16,16,11,18,15,13,15,13,11,13,10,12]
df = moving_average(d)
```

Visualization with pandas

You can easily plot any DataFrame simply by calling the method .plot() on it. Typically, if you want to plot the demand and the forecast we just made, you can simply type

```
df[["Demand","Forecast"]].plot()
```

You can also customize .plot() by specifying some parameters.

figsize(width,height) defines the size of the figure. Dimensions are given in inches.
title displays a title if given.

---

[1] nan stands for not a number.

ylim=(min,max) it allows us to determine the range of the y axis of our plot.

style=[] this allows us to define the style of each of the lines that are plotted. "-" will be a continuous line whereas "--" will be a discontinous line.

Here's an example:

```
df[["Demand","Forecast"]].plot(figsize=(8,3),title="Moving average",ylim
    =(0,30),style=["-","--"])
```

By default, `.plot()` will use the `DataFrame index` as the x axis. Therefore, if you want to display a legend on the x axis, you simply can name the `DataFrame index`.

```
df.index.name = "Periods"
```

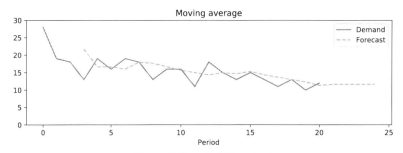

Figure 1.3: `.plot()` output

- As you can see on this plot, the future forecast (as of period 20) is flat. As discussed, this is due to the fact that this moving average model does not *see* a trend and therefore can't project any.

Chapter 2

Forecast Error

Now that we have created our first forecast model, we need to quantify its accuracy. As you will see, measuring forecast accuracy (or error) is not an easy task as **there is no one-size-fits-all indicator**. Only experimentation will show you what Key Performance Indicator (KPI) is best for you. As you will see, each indicator will avoid some pitfalls but will be prone to others.

The first distinction we have to make is the difference between the precision of a forecast and its bias:

> **Bias** represents the historical average error. Basically, will your forecasts be on average too high (i.e. you *overshot* the demand) or too low (i.e. you *undershot* the demand)? This will give you the overall direction of the error.
>
> **Precision** measures how much spread you will have between the forecast and the actual value. The precision of a forecast gives an idea of the magnitude of the errors but not their overall direction.

Of course, as you can see on figure 2.1, what we want to have is a forecast that is both precise and unbiased.

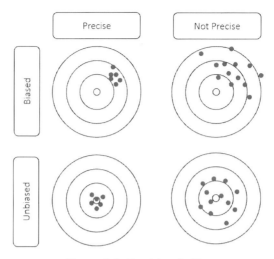

Figure 2.1: Precision & Bias

Forecast KPI

Error

Let's start by defining the error as the forecast minus the demand.

$$e_t = f_t - d_t$$

Note that with this definition, if the forecast overshoots the demand, the error will be positive and if the forecast undershoots the demand, then the error will be negative.

Bias

The bias is defined as the average error.

$$bias = \frac{1}{n} \sum_n e_t$$

Where *n* is the number of historical periods where you have both a forecast and a demand.
As a positive error on one item can offset a negative error on another item, a forecast model can achieve a very low bias and not be precise at the same time. Obviously, the bias alone won't be enough to evaluate your

Forecast KPI

forecast precision. But a highly biased forecast is already an indication that something is wrong in the model.

MAPE

The **Mean Absolute Percentage Error** (or MAPE) is one of the most commonly used KPIs to measure forecast accuracy. MAPE is the sum of the individual absolute errors divided by the demand (each period separately). Actually, it is the average of the percentage errors.

$$MAPE = \frac{1}{n} \sum \frac{|e_t|}{d_t}$$

MAPE is a really strange forecast KPI.

It is quite well-known among business managers, despite being a really poor-accuracy indicator. As you can see in the formula, MAPE divides each error individually by the demand, so it is skewed: high errors during low-demand periods will have a major impact on MAPE. Due to this, optimizing MAPE will result in a strange forecast that will most likely undershoot the demand. Just avoid it.

MAE

The **Mean Absolute Error** (MAE) is a very good KPI to measure forecast accuracy. As the name implies, it is the mean of the absolute error.

$$MAE = \frac{1}{n} \sum |e_t|$$

One of the first issues of this KPI is that it is not scaled to the average demand. If one tells you that MAE is 10 for a particular item, you cannot know if this is good or bad. If your average demand is 1000, it is of course astonishing, but if the average demand is 1, this is a very poor accuracy. To solve this, it is common to divide MAE by the average demand to get a %:

$$MAE\% = \frac{\frac{1}{n} \sum |e_t|}{\frac{1}{n} \sum d_t} = \frac{\sum |e_t|}{\sum d_t}$$

MAPE/MAE Confusion It seems that many practitioners use the MAE formula and call it MAPE. This can cause a lot of confusion. When discussing forecast error with someone, I would always advise you to explicitly show how you compute the forecast error to be sure to compare apples and apples.

RMSE

The **Root Mean Square Error** (RMSE) is a strange KPI but a very helpful one as we will discuss later. It is defined as the square root of the average squared error.

$$RMSE = \sqrt{\frac{1}{n}\sum e_t^2}$$

Just as for MAE, RMSE is not scaled to the demand. We can then define RMSE% as such,

$$RMSE\% = \frac{\sqrt{\frac{1}{n}\sum e_t^2}}{\frac{\sum d}{n}}$$

Actually, many algorithms (especially for machine learning) are based on the **Mean Square Error** (MSE), which is directly related to RMSE.

$$MSE = \frac{1}{n}\sum e_t^2$$

MSE is used by many algorithms as it is faster to compute and easier to manipulate than RMSE. But it is not scaled to the original error (as the error is squared), resulting in a KPI that we cannot really relate to the original demand scale. Therefore, we won't use it to evaluate our statistical forecast models.

A question of error weighting

Compared to MAE, RMSE does not treat each error the same. It gives more importance to the biggest errors. That means that one big error is enough to get a very bad RMSE.

Let's do an example with a dummy demand time series.

Period	1	2	3	4	5	6	7	8	9	10	11	12
Demand	10	12	14	8	9	5	8	10	12	11	10	15

Let's imagine we want to compare two slightly different forecasts. The only difference is the forecast on the latest demand observation: forecast #1 undershot it by 7 units and forecast #2 by *only* 6 units.

Period	1	2	3	4	5	6	7	8	9	10	11	**12**
Demand	10	12	14	8	9	5	8	10	12	11	10	**15**
Forecast #1	12	14	15	10	7	4	5	8	12	14	13	**8**
Error #1	2	2	1	2	-2	-1	-3	-2	0	3	3	**-7**
Forecast #2	12	14	15	10	7	4	5	8	12	14	13	**9**
Error #2	2	2	1	2	-2	-1	-3	-2	0	3	3	**-6**

If we look at the KPI of these two forecasts, this is what we obtain:

KPI	MAE	RMSE
Forecast #1	2.33	2.86
Forecast #2	2.25	2.66

What is interesting here is that by just changing the error of this last period by a single unit, we decrease the total RMSE by 6.9% (2.86 to 2.66) but MAE is only reduced by 3.6% (2.33 to 2.25), so the impact on MAE is nearly twice as low. Clearly RMSE puts much more importance on the biggest errors whereas MAE gives the same importance to each error. You can try this for yourself and reduce the error of one of the most accurate periods to observe the impact on MAE and RMSE.

Spoiler: nearly no impact on RMSE.

As you will see later, RMSE has some other very interesting properties.

What would you like to predict?

We went through the definition of these KPIs (bias, MAPE, MAE, RMSE) but it is still unclear what difference it can make for our model to use one instead of another. One could think that using RMSE instead of MAE, or MAE instead of MAPE doesn't change anything. But nothing is less true.

Let's do a quick example to show this. Let's imagine a product with a low and rather flat weekly demand that has from time to time a big order (maybe due to promotions, or to clients ordering in batches). Here is the demand per week that we observed so far:

	W1	W2	W3	W4	W5
Mon	3	3	4	1	5
Tue	1	4	1	2	2
Wed	5	5	1	1	12
Thu	20	4	3	2	1
Fri	13	16	14	5	20

Now let's imagine we propose 3 different forecasts for this product. The first one predicts 2 pieces/day, the second one 4 and the last one 6. Let's plot the demand we observed and these forecasts.

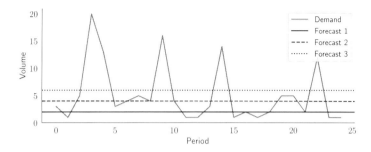

Let's see how each of these forecasts performs in terms of bias, MAPE, MAE and RMSE on the historical period:

	Forecast 1	Forecast 2	Forecast 3
Bias	-3.9	-1.9	**0.1**
MAPE	**64%**	109%	180%
MAE	4.4	**4.1**	4.8
RMSE	7.1	6.2	**5.9**

It means that forecast #1 was the best during the historical period in terms of MAPE, forecast #2 was the best in terms of MAE and forecast #3 was the best in terms of RMSE and bias (but the worst on MAE and MAPE). Let's now reveal how these forecasts were made:

Forecast 1 is just a very low amount.
Forecast 2 is the demand median[1]: 4.
Forecast 3 is the average demand.

Median vs Average – mathematical optimization

Before discussing the different forecast KPIs further, let's take some time to understand why a forecast of the median will get a good MAE and a forecast of the mean a good RMSE.

There is a bit of maths ahead If these equations are unclear to you, this is not an issue – don't get discouraged. Just skip them and jump to the conclusion of the **RMSE** and **MAE** paragraphs.

---

[1] The median is the value for which half the dataset is higher and half of the dataset is lower.

RMSE

Let's start with RMSE:

$$RMSE = \sqrt{\frac{1}{n}\sum e_t^2}$$

Actually, to simplify the following algebra, let's use a simplified version: the Mean Squared Error (MSE):

$$MSE = \frac{1}{n}\sum e_t^2$$

If you set MSE as a target for your forecast model, it will minimize it. One can minimize a mathematical function by setting its derivative to zero. Let's try this.

$$\frac{\partial MSE}{\partial f} = \frac{\partial \frac{1}{n}\sum(f_t - d_t)^2}{\partial f}$$

$$\frac{2}{n}\sum(f_t - d_t) = 0$$

$$\sum f_t = \sum d_t$$

Conclusion to optimize a forecast's MSE, the model will have to aim for the total forecast to be equal to the total demand. That is to say that optimizing MSE aims to produce a prediction that is correct *on average* and therefore unbiased.

MAE

Now let's do the same for MAE.

$$\frac{\partial MAE}{\partial f} = \frac{\partial \frac{1}{n}\sum |f_t - d_t|}{\partial f}$$

Or,

$$|f_t - d_t| = \begin{cases} f_t - d_t & d_t < f_t \\ indefinite & d_t = f_t \\ d_t - f_t & d_t > f_t \end{cases}$$

and

$$\frac{\partial |f_t - d_t|}{\partial f} = \begin{cases} 1 & d_t < f_t \\ indefinite & d_t = f_t \\ -1 & d_t > f_t \end{cases}$$

Which means that

$$\frac{\partial MAE}{\partial f} = \frac{1}{n}\sum \begin{cases} 1 & d_t < f_t \\ -1 & d_t > f_t \end{cases}$$

Conclusion to optimize MAE (i.e. set its derivative to 0), the forecast needs to be as many times higher than the demand as it is lower than the demand. In other words, we are looking for a value that splits our dataset into two equal parts. This is the exact definition of the median.

MAPE

Unfortunately, the derivative of MAPE won't show some elegant and straightforward property. We can simply say that MAPE is promoting a very low forecast as it allocates a high weight to forecast errors when the demand is low.

Conclusion

As we saw above, in any model, the optimization of RMSE will seek to be correct on average whereas the optimization of MAE will try to be as often overshooting the demand as undershooting the demand, which means targeting the demand median. We have to understand that a big difference lies at the mathematical roots of MAE & RMSE. **One aims at the median, the second aims at the average.**

MAE or RMSE – which one to choose?

Is it worse to aim for the median or the average of the demand? Well, the answer is not black and white. Each technique has some benefits and some risks, as we will discuss in the next pages. Only experimentation will reveal which technique works best for a dataset. You can even choose to use both RMSE & MAE.

Let's take some time to discuss the impact of choosing either RMSE or MAE on the bias, the sensitivity to outliers and the intermittent demand.

Bias

For many products, you will observe that the median is not the same as the average demand. Most likely, the demand will have some peaks here and there that will result in a skewed distribution. These skewed demand distributions are very common in supply chain as the peaks can be due to periodic promotions or clients ordering in bulk. This will cause the demand median to be below the average demand, as shown on figure 2.2.

What would you like to predict?

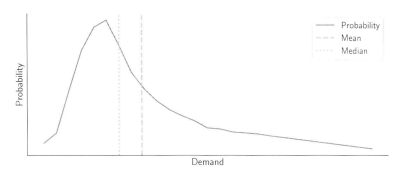

Figure 2.2: Median vs Average

This means that a forecast that is minimizing MAE **will result in a bias**. Whereas a forecast that is minimizing RMSE will not result in a bias (as it aims for the average). This is definitely MAE's main weakness.

Sensitivity to outliers

As we discussed, RMSE gives a bigger importance to the highest errors. This comes at a cost: a sensitivity to outliers. Let's imagine an item with the following demand pattern.

Period	1	2	3	4	5	6	7	8	9	10
Demand	16	8	12	9	6	12	5	7	6	14

The median is 8.5 and the average is 9.5. We already observed that if we make a forecast that minimizes MAE, we will forecast the median (8.5) and we would be on average undershooting the demand by 1 unit (bias = -1). You might then prefer to minimize RMSE and to forecast the average (9.5) to avoid this situation. Nevertheless, let's now imagine that we have one new demand observation of 100.

Period	1	2	3	4	5	6	7	8	9	10
Demand	16	8	12	9	6	12	5	7	6	**100**

The median is still 8.5 (it hasn't changed!) but the average is now **18.1**. In this case, you might not want to forecast the average and might revert back to a forecast of the median.

Generally speaking, the median is more robust to outliers than the average. In a supply chain environment, this is rather important as we can face many outliers due to encoding mistakes or demand peaks (marketing, promotions, spot deals).

Is robustness to outliers always a good thing? No.

Intermittent demand

Indeed, unfortunately, the median's robustness to outliers can result in a very annoying effect for items with an intermittent demand.

Let's imagine that we sell a product to a single client. It is a highly profitable product and our unique client seems to make an order one week out of three. Unfortunately, without any kind of pattern. The client always orders the product by batches of 100. We then have an average weekly demand of 33 pieces and a demand median of... 0.

We have to populate a weekly forecast for this product. Let's imagine we do a first forecast that aims for the average demand (33 pieces). Over the long-term, we will obtain a total squared error of 6 667 (RMSE of 47) and a total absolute error of 133 (MAE of 44).

Week	Demand	Forecast	Error	|Error|	Error^2
1	100	33	67	67	4 445
2	0	33	-33	33	1 111
3	0	33	-33	33	1 111
Total	100	100	0	133	6 667

Now, if we forecast the demand median (0), we obtain a total absolute error of 100 (MAE of 33) and a total squared error of 10.000 (RMSE of 58).

Week	Demand	Forecast	Error	|Error|	Error^2
1	100	0	-100	100	10 000
2	0	0	0	0	0
3	0	0	0	0	0
Total	100	0	-100	100	10 000

As we can see, MAE is a bad KPI to use for intermittent demand. As soon as you have more than half of the periods without demand, the optimal forecast is... 0!

Conclusion

MAE provides a protection against outliers whereas RMSE provides the assurance to get an unbiased forecast. Which indicator should you use?

What would you like to predict?

There is unfortunately no definitive answer. As a supply chain data scientist, you should experiment: if using MAE as a KPI results in a high bias, you might want to use RMSE. If the dataset contains many outliers, resulting in a skewed forecast, you might want to use MAE.

Note as well that you can choose to report forecast error with one or more KPIs (typically MAE & bias) and use another one (RMSE?) to optimize your models.

A last trick to use against low-demand items is to aggregate the demand to a higher time horizon. For example, if the demand is low at a weekly level, you could test a monthly forecast or even a quarterly forecast. You can always disaggregate the forecast back into the original time bucket by simply dividing it. This technique can allow you to use MAE as a KPI and smooth demand peaks at the same time.

Chapter 3

Exponential Smoothing

Idea

A simple exponential smoothing is one of the simplest ways to forecast a time series. The basic idea of this model is to assume that the future will be more or less the same as the (recent) past. The only pattern that this model will be able to learn from demand history is its level.

The **level** is the average value around which the demand varies over time. As you can observe on figure 3.1, the level is a smoothed version of the demand.

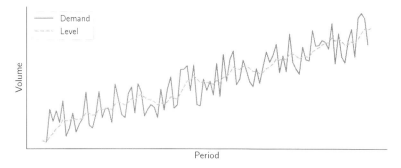

Figure 3.1: Demand level

The exponential smoothing model will then forecast the future demand as its last estimation of the level. It is important to understand that there is no definitive mathematical definition of the level, instead it is up to our model to **estimate** it.

The exponential smoothing model will have some advantages compared to a naïve or a moving average model (see chapter 1):

- The weight that is put on each observation decreases **exponentially**[1] over time (the most recent observation has the highest weight). This is often better than moving average models where the same weight is given to all the relevant historical months.
- Outliers and noise have less impact than with the naïve method.

Model

The underlying idea of any exponential smoothing model is that, at each period, the model will learn a bit from the most recent demand observation and remember a bit of the last forecast it did. The magic about this is that the last forecast the model did was including a part of the previous demand observation and a part of the previous forecast. And so forth. **That means that this previous forecast actually includes everything the model learned so far based on demand history**. The smoothing parameter (or learning rate) **alpha** (α) will determine how much importance is given to the most recent demand observation. Let's represent this mathematically,

$$f_t = \alpha d_{t-1} + (1-\alpha)f_{t-1}$$

$$0 < \alpha \leq 1$$

What is the intuition behind this formula?

α is a ratio (or a percentage) of how much importance the model will allocate to the most recent observation compared to the importance of demand history.

αd_{t-1} represents the previous demand observation times the learning rate. You could say that the model attaches a certain importance (alpha) to the last demand occurrence.

$(1-\alpha)f_{t-1}$ represents how much the model remembers from its previous forecast. Note that this is where the recursive magic happens as f_{t-1} was itself defined as partially d_{t-2} and f_{t-2}.

---

[1]We'll discuss this in more details on page 31.

Model

There is an important trade-off to be made here between *learning* and *remembering*; between being reactive and being stable. If alpha is high, the model will allocate more importance to the most recent demand observation (i.e. the model will learn fast) and it will be reactive to a change in the demand level. But it will also be sensitive to outliers and noise. On the other hand if alpha is low, the model won't notice a change in level rapidly, but will also not overreact to noise and outliers.

Future forecast

Once we are out of the historical period, we need to populate a forecast for the future periods. This is simple: the last forecast (the one based on the most recent demand observation) is simply extrapolated into the future. If we define f_{t*} as the last forecast that we could make based on demand history, we simply have

$$f_{t>t*} = f_{t*}$$

Model initialization

As with every model, the question comes of the initialization of the first forecast. This simple question unfortunately does not have a simple answer. Actually, this will often be the case in this book: the simplest questions won't always have definitive and absolute answers. As we will discuss over and over, only experimentation will allow us to understand which technique works best for each dataset. Let's discuss some ideas.

Simple initialization   We initialize the first forecast (period 0) as the first demand observation. We then have

$$f_0 = d_0$$

This is a simple & fair way to initialize the forecast.

Average   We initialize the forecast as the average of the first *n* demand occurrences.

$$f_0 = \frac{1}{n} \sum_{t=0}^{n} d_t$$

In such a case, I would advise to test different values of *n*. It could either be set as a fixed small value (3 to 5) or as the inverse of the learning rate ($\frac{1}{\alpha}$). If *n* is set as the inverse of the learning rate, this allows a smoother estimation of f_0 as the learning rate decreases. This makes sense as a low value for α means that we want our model to react smoothly to variations.

Data leakage

If you choose an initialization method that includes information about multiple periods ahead — for example if you define the initial forecast as the average of the first five periods — you face a **data leakage**. This means that you provide your model with pieces of information about the future. Basically, you tell it: *"Can you provide me a forecast of the next period, knowing that the average of the demand for the next five periods is 10?"*. This is a typical example of overfitting (as we will discuss in details in chapter 8): the model will give you a good forecast accuracy for the initial periods (that's easy — you gave it the average demand of theses periods!), but won't be able to replicate such accuracy in the future.

Always be cautious when you initialize the different parameters of a model not to give it too much information about the future.

Insights

Impact of α

On figure 3.2, we see that a forecast made with a low alpha value (here 0.1) will take more time to react to a changing demand, whereas a forecast with a high alpha value (here 0.8) will follow closely the demand fluctuations.

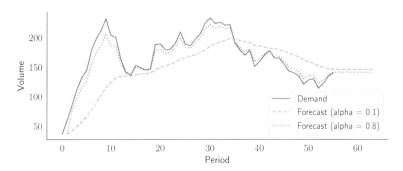

Figure 3.2: Simple smoothing

Why is it called exponential smoothing?

This model is called exponential smoothing as the weight given to each demand observation is exponentially reduced. To show this, we will start by taking back the exponential smoothing model.

$$f_t = \alpha d_{t-1} + (1-\alpha)f_{t-1}$$

As you can see, the weight given to the most recent demand observation d_{t-1} is α. Now let's replace f_{t-1} by its formula.

$$f_t = \alpha d_{t-1} + (1-\alpha)f_{t-1}$$
$$= \alpha d_{t-1} + (1-\alpha)\Big(\alpha d_{t-2} + (1-\alpha)f_{t-2}\Big)$$

If we do a bit of algebra, we obtain the following formula:

$$f_t = \alpha d_{t-1} + \alpha(1-\alpha)d_{t-2} + (1-\alpha)^2 f_{t-2}$$

We see that the weight given to the second most recent demand observation d_{t-2} is $\alpha(1-\alpha)$, which is lower than the weight given to d_{t-1}. Let's go further and replace f_{t-2} by its formula.

$$f_t = \alpha d_{t-1} + \alpha(1-\alpha)d_{t-2} + (1-\alpha)^2\Big(\alpha d_{t-3} + (1-\alpha)f_{t-3}\Big)$$
$$= \alpha d_{t-1} + \alpha(1-\alpha)d_{t-2} + \alpha(1-\alpha)^2 d_{t-3} + (1-\alpha)^3 f_{t-3}$$

We see that the weight given to d_{t-3} is $\alpha(1-\alpha)^2$; which is the weight given to d_{t-2} multiplied by $(1-\alpha)$. From here, we deduce that the weight given to each further demand observation is reduced by a factor $(1-\alpha)$. This is why we call this method **exponential** smoothing.

Period	Moving Average n					Exponential Smoothing α				
	5	4	3	2	1	0.2	0.4	0.6	0.8	1
$t-1$	0.2	0.25	0.33	0.5	1	0.20	0.40	0.60	0.80	1
$t-2$	0.2	0.25	0.33	0.5		0.16	0.24	0.24	0.16	
$t-3$	0.2	0.25	0.33			0.13	0.14	0.10	0.03	
$t-4$	0.2	0.25				0.10	0.09	0.04	0.01	
$t-5$	0.2					0.08	0.05	0.02		

Table 3.1: Weight allocated to each historical period

Limitations

This simple exponential smoothing model is slightly smarter than the moving average model thanks to its smarter weighting of the historical demand observation. But it has many limitations:

- It does not project trends. We will solve this with our next model: the exponential smoothing with trend, otherwise known as **double exponential smoothing**.
- It does not recognize any seasonal pattern. We will solve this with the **triple exponential smoothing** model.
- It cannot use any external information (such as pricing or marketing expenses).

In conclusion, this first exponential smoothing model will be most likely too simple to achieve good results, but it is a good foundation block to create more complex models later.

A brief history of Holt-Winters models

The exponential smoothing models are often called "Holt-Winters", based on the names of the researchers who proposed these models. Actually, an early form of exponential smoothing forecast was initially proposed by R.G. Brown in 1956. His equations were refined in 1957 by Charles C. Holt — a US engineer from the MIT and the University of Chicago — in his paper "Forecasting Trends and Seasonals by Exponentially Weighted Averages" [7]. The exponential smoothing models were again improved 3 years later by Peter Winters [13]. Their two names were remembered and given to the different exponential smoothing techniques that we sometimes call "Holt-Winters".

Holt & Winters actually proposed different exponential smoothing models (simple, double and triple) that can also understand & project a trend or a seasonality. This ensemble of models is then quite robust to forecast any time series. And, as Holt and Winters already explained in 1960, these forecasts only require a modest use of computation power.

Do It Yourself

Excel

1. We start our data table by creating three columns:
    Date on **column A**
    Demand on **column B**
    Forecast on **column C**

Do It Yourself

2. Next to this, let's add a cell with alpha (F1 in our example). Don't forget to clearly indicate that this cell is alpha.
3. Once this is done, you can initialize the first forecast (cell C2) as the first demand (cell B2).

	A	B	C	D	E	F
1	Date	Demand	Forecast		Alpha:	10%
2	1	37	37			
3	2	60				
4	3	85				
5	4	112				
6	5	132				
7	6	145				
8	7	179				
9	8	198				
10	9	212				
11	10	232				
12	11					

4. We can now populate our forecast; as of cell C3, we can use this formula:

$$C3=\$F\$1*B2+(1-\$F\$1)*C2$$

	A	B	C	D	E	F
1	Date	Demand	Forecast		Alpha:	10%
2	1	37	37			
3	2	60	=$F$1*B2+			

5. To continue our forecast until the end of the historical period, we can simply drag this formula until the end of the table.
6. All the future forecasts (i.e. the forecasts out of the historical period), will simply be equivalent to the very last forecast based on historical demand (as shown on figure 3.3).

Exponential Smoothing

	A	B	C
1	Date	Demand	Forecast
2	1	37	37
3	2	60	37
4	3	85	39
5	4	112	44
6	5	132	51
7	6	145	59
8	7	179	67
9	8	198	79
10	9	212	91
11	10	232	103
12	11		=C11
13	12		103
14	13		103

Figure 3.3: Future forecast

Python

Simple smoothing function

We will define a function `simple_exp_smooth` that takes a time series d as input and returns a `pandas DataFrame df` with the historical demand, the forecast and the error. The function also takes `extra_periods` as an input, which is the number of periods that need to be forecast into the future. The last input is the alpha parameter.

```python
def simple_exp_smooth(d,extra_periods=1,alpha=0.4):

    # Transform the input into a numpy array
    d = np.array(d)
    # Historical period length
    cols = len(d)
    # Append np.nan into the demand array to cover future periods
    d = np.append(d,[np.nan]*extra_periods)

    # Forecast array
    f = np.full(cols+extra_periods,np.nan)
    # initialization of first forecast
    f[1] = d[0]

    # Create all the t+1 forecasts until end of historical period
    for t in range(2,cols+1):
        f[t] = alpha*d[t-1]+(1-alpha)*f[t-1]
```

Do It Yourself

```
18
19      # Forecast for all extra periods
20      f[cols+1:] = f[t]
21
22      df = pd.DataFrame.from_dict({"Demand":d,"Forecast":f,"Error":d-f})
23
24      return df
```

Playing with our function

We can then simply call our function (here with a dummy demand time series):

```
1  import numpy as np
2  import pandas as pd
3  d=[28,19,18,13,19,16,19,18,13,16,16,11,18,15,13,15,13,11,13,10,12]
4  df = simple_exp_smooth(d,extra_periods=4)
```

You can also easily get the forecast accuracy with simple commands such as shown below.

```
1  MAE = df["Error"].abs().mean()
2  print("MAE:",round(MAE,2))
3  RMSE = np.sqrt((df["Error"]**2).mean())
4  print("RMSE:",round(RMSE,2))
```

```
1  MAE: 2.74
2  RMSE: 3.89
```

Another very interesting step is to plot the results in order to analyse how the model behaves. You can see the results on figure 3.4.

```
1  df.index.name = "Periods"
2  df[["Demand","Forecast"]].plot(figsize=(8,3),title="Simple Smoothing",ylim
      =(0,30),style=["-","--"])
```

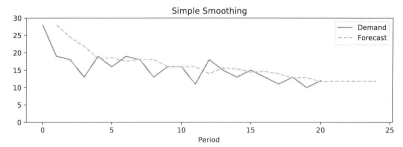

Figure 3.4: Example of simple smoothing forecast

Chapter 4

Underfitting

> *All models are wrong, but some are helpful*
> George Box (1919 – 2013)

A model aims to describe reality. As reality can be rather complex, a model will be built on some assumptions (i.e. simplifications), as summarized by statistician George Box. Unfortunately, some forecast models (due to these assumptions or some limitations) will not be able to properly predict or explain the reality they are built upon.

We say that a model is **underfitted** if it does not explain reality properly enough.

To analyze the abilities of our model, we will divide our dataset (i.e. the historical demand in the case of forecast) into two different parts:

Training dataset this is the dataset that we use to train (or "fit") our model (i.e. optimize its parameters). Typically, in the case of forecast models, we use historical demand as the training dataset in order to optimize the different parameters (α for the simple exponential smoothing model).

Test dataset this dataset will help us assess the accuracy of our model against **unseen** data. In order to do so, we will keep the test set aside to test our model once it is fitted to the training dataset. That means that we will not use the test set to train our model. Typically, to test our forecast, we could keep the latest periods out of the training dataset, to see how our model would have behaved during these periods.

We need to be very careful with our test set. We can never use it to optimize our model. Keep in mind that this dataset is here to show us how our model would perform against new data. If we optimize our model on the test dataset, we will never know what accuracy we can expect against new demand.

One could say that an underfitted model lacks a good understanding of the training dataset. As the model does not perform properly on the training dataset, it will not perform well on the test set either. In the case of demand forecasting, it means that a model that does not achieve a good accuracy on historical demand will not perform properly on future demand either.

We will now look into two possible reasons for underfitting and how to solve these cases.

Cause of underfitting

Model complexity

The first possible reason for underfitting (i.e. the model does not achieve satisfying results on the training dataset) is that its inner complexity is too low. One could say that the model lacks the ability to learn the appropriate patterns from the historical dataset.

On figure 4.1, you can see a dummy dataset of demand points that follows a noisy quadratic curve ($y = -x^2$). On top of this, you see two models that we fitted to this dataset. The first one is a linear regression and the second one an exponential smoothing.

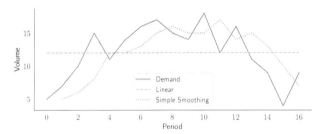

Figure 4.1: Linear regression vs Simple smoothing

We see that the linear model fits this historical demand poorly (with an RMSE of 34%). Most likely, if we used this model to predict the demand

Cause of underfitting

over the next periods – which is likely to be close to zero – the model would fail and continue to predict the average historical demand.

The forecast made with a simple exponential smoothing model is achieving a much better fit on the historical dataset: it has an RMSE of 30%. We observe that this model understands that the demand level changes over time and we can then expect this model to behave better on future demand. The linear model was simply not complex enough to understand the relationship behind the data.

Lack of explanatory variables

Let's imagine another case where you sell ice cream near a school. The sales are rather high during the week and much lower during the weekend. Let's plot this situation and a first simple exponential smoothing forecast.

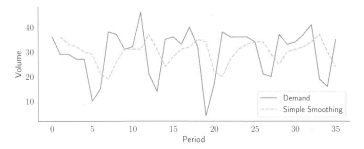

Figure 4.2: Ice cream consumption

We see that our simple exponential smoothing is absolutely not adapted to this demand pattern. The model over-forecasts the weekends and then under-forecasts the first weekdays. We will see later (in chapter 9) a perfect model for this situation: a seasonal exponential smoothing model. But for now, let's just imagine a model that understands the difference between a weekday and the weekend. To do this, we will use two different models: one will forecast weekdays and the other one weekends. Both of these will be simple exponential smoothing models.

With our new model duo, we fit the demand much better (as shown on figure 4.3) as our model understands that weekdays and weekends are not the same. In other words, our model has a new explanatory variable: *"Is it a weekday?"*. The initial model (the simple exponential smoothing)

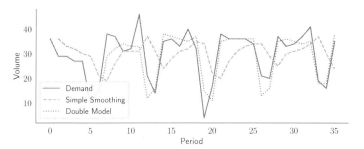

Figure 4.3: Double model vs Simple smoothing

simply didn't get the information of weekends/weekdays difference, so that it cannot understand the underlying relationship.

In many industries, we could have similar stories with pricing and marketing: high demand during periods with promotions or advertisement and otherwise lower demand. In such cases, a model that does not take these factors into account will fail to properly predict the demand. Unfortunately, exponential smoothing models are not able to take these explanatory variables into account. We will discuss how to integrate these exogenous variables in our forecast in chapter 20, once we have powerfull machine learning models in our toolbox.

Solutions

We have identified a typical problem with (predictive) models: **underfitting**. That is to say that the model is not smart enough to understand the relationships present in the training data. Two solutions can be used to increase its predictive abilities:

- Use more explanatory variables (such as weekdays/weekends, marketing expenses, pricing)
- Change the model for a more complex one (add a trend, a seasonality)

As a final piece of advice, don't use your model to predict future demand if it does not perform well on the historical dataset.

Chapter 5

Double Exponential Smoothing

> *When the facts change, I change my mind. What do you do, sir?*
> John Maynard Keynes

Idea

We saw with the simple exponential smoothing algorithm that we could create a simple forecast that assumed that the future of the demand time series would be similar to its past. A major issue of this simple smoothing was its inability to identify and project a **trend**.

We define the **trend** as the average variation of the time series level between two consecutive periods. Remember that the level was the average value around which the demand varies over time.

If you assume that your time series follows a trend, most likely you will not know its magnitude in advance. Especially as this magnitude could vary over time. This is fine, as we will create a model that will learn *by itself* the trend over time. Just as for the level, this new model will estimate the trend based on an exponential weight **beta** (β), giving more or less importance to the most recent observations.

Model

The general idea behind exponential smoothing models is that each component (here the level and the trend, later the seasonality as well) will be updated at each period based on two pieces of information:

1. the **most recent observation** of this component;
2. The **previous estimation** of this component.

Remember that for the simple exponential smoothing model, we updated the forecast at each period partially based on the previous demand (i.e. the most recent observation of this component) and partially based on the previous forecast (i.e. the previous estimation of this component). We will now do the same for the level (noted a_t) and the trend (noted b_t).

Level estimation Let's see how the model will estimate the level:

$$a_t = \alpha d_t + (1-\alpha)(a_{t-1} + b_{t-1})$$

This should look familiar: it is the same logic as the forecast for the simple exponential smoothing. The model will update its estimation of the level a_t at each period thanks to two pieces of information: the last demand observation d_t and the previous level estimation increased by the trend $a_{t-1} + b_{t-1}$ (remember we assume the level to change by the trend at each period).

Trend estimation The model will also have to estimate the trend. In order to do so, we will apply a similar logic:

$$b_t = \beta(a_t - a_{t-1}) + (1-\beta)b_{t-1}$$

β is the new learning parameter for the trend. Just as α for the level, it represents how much weight is given to the most recent level observation: $a_t - a_{t-1}$ (i.e. the difference between the last two levels). $(1-\beta)$ is the importance given to the previous trend estimation b_{t-1}.

Forecast Finally, we simply set the forecast for period $t+1$ as

$$f_{t+1} = a_t + b_t$$

Or, to be more general (for a forecast of period $t+\lambda$),

$$f_{t+\lambda} = a_t + \lambda b_t$$

Model

Future forecast As soon as we are out of the historical period, we simply forecast each period as the last forecast plus the trend, using the general future forecast formula above. We also note that if $t*$ is the latest period for which we know the demand, we obtain:

$$f_{t*+\lambda} = a_{t*} + \lambda b_{t*}$$

That basically means that the model will extrapolate the latest trend it could observe. As we will see later, this might unfortunately be a problem.

Model initialization

Just like the forecast initialization of the simple exponential smoothing, we have to discuss how to initialize the first estimations of our level and trend (a_0 & b_0). As often, simple questions don't have simple absolute answers. Only experimentation will tell you what initialization works best in your case.

Simple initialization

We can initialize the level and the trend simply based on $a_0 = d_0$ and $b_0 = d_1 - d_0$. This is a simple and fair initialization method. You have a limited data leakage (see page 30) but the initial forecast is entirely dependant on the first two demand observations.

Note that if we do this, the first forecast f_1 will be perfect, as

$$\begin{aligned} f_1 &= a_0 + b_0 \\ &= d_0 + (d_1 - d_0) \\ &= d_1 \end{aligned}$$

As the first forecast (f_1) will be perfect, you will give an unfair advantage in terms of accuracy to this initialization method compared to any other method[1]. On big datasets, this is fine — as you only improve one prediction over many — but on smaller sets, this advantage might result in overfitting (as we will discuss later, in chapter 8).

Linear regression

Another way to initialize a_0 & b_0 would be to do a linear regression of the first n demand observations. Again, n could be defined as an arbitrarily

---
[1] The initialization of the forecast can be interpreted as *"Can you forecast tomorrow, knowing that we are going to sell 5 today and 10 units more tomorrow?"*

rather low number (e.g. 3 or 5) or as something proportional to the average of $\frac{1}{\beta}$ and $\frac{1}{\alpha}$. Pay attention that as *n* grows, the data leakage becomes more important.

How to do linear regressions is out of scope for this book. Nevertheless, you can take a look at the function np.polyfit(x,y,deg=1) in Python or LINEST() in Excel. You can also do a linear regression analysis in Excel if you activate the add-on Data Analysis (the procedure is similar to the one of the solver – see page 56). Once it is activated, you can launch it by going to the ribbon to Data/Analysis/Data Analysis and then select Regression in the menu.

Insights

Let's plot a first example with rather low α (0.2) and β (0.4).

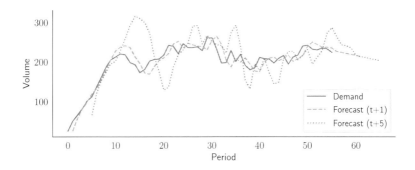

We made two forecasts, one for period $t+1$ and another one for $t+5$. The forecast at $t+1$ is rather good (as expected), but we observe that the forecast at $t+5$ can get wrong due to the trend extrapolation (look at periods 10–20).

Trend & error

There is an interesting relationship between the forecast error and the trend. As you can observe on figure 5.1, the trend decreases when the error is positive. And the trend increases when the error is negative. The intuition is that our model learns from its mistakes. Not everyone is able to do this... If the model undershot the last demand, it will increase the trend. If it overshot the last demand, it will decrease the trend.

Insights

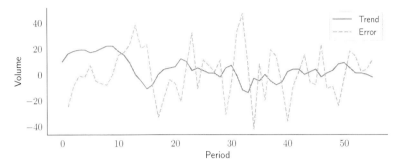

Figure 5.1: Trend & error

There is now a real temptation: shouldn't we increase the trend learning rate, so that the model would learn faster from its previous mistakes? We are supply chain data scientists, so let's experiment and try a model powered by high learning rates (α and β set to 0.8).

This is what we get.

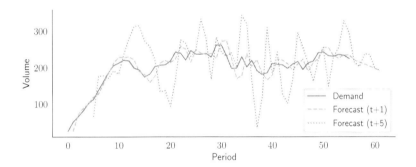

We now see that the forecast at $t+5$ starts to oscillate around the demand. This is very bad — even dangerous! — for a supply chain, as it will most likely result in a bullwhip effect[1]. We will discuss in the next chapters how to properly set the learning parameters.

Model analysis

Exponential smoothing models are very useful as they allow us to **understand** a forecast or a time series thanks to the decomposition they do

---

[1] The bullwhip effect is observed in supply chains where small variations in the downstream demand result in massive variations in the upstream supply chain.

between the level and the trend (and, as we will see later, the seasonality). One can check the state of any of the demand sub-components at any point in time. Exactly like if you could inspect what is happening under the hood of the model.

Do not hesitate to plot these different components to understand how your model *sees* (or *understands*) a specific product (see figure 5.2 for an example). This will explain you why your model forecasts a specific value.

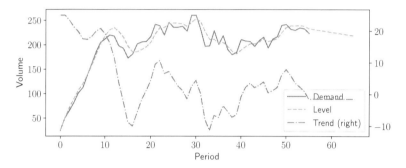

Figure 5.2: Level & trend components

The value of the different smoothing parameters (α and β for now; ϕ and γ later) will also tell you something about the variability or smoothness of your product. High values will denote a product where each variation should have an impact on the forecast; low values will denote products with a more constant behaviour that shouldn't be impacted by short-term fluctuations.

As we will discuss in the second part of the book, it is very unfortunate that machine learning models won't provide us this kind of understanding or interpretation of a time series' sub-components. This is one of the reasons why exponential smoothing models are complementary to machine learning.

Limitations

Our double exponential smoothing model is now able to recognize a trend and extrapolate it into the future. This is a major improvement compared to simple exponential smoothing (or moving average). But, unfortunately, this comes with a risk...

> *In 50 years, every street in London will be buried under nine feet of manure.*
> The Times (1894)

Our model will assume that the trend will go on forever[1]. This might result in some issues for mid/long-term forecasts. We will solve this thanks to the damped trend model (page 61) – a model that was only published 25 years later, in 1985!

Next to this risk of infinite trend, we still have

- The lack of seasonality. This will be solved via the triple exponential smoothing model.
- The impossibility to take external information into account (like marketing budget or price variations).

Do It Yourself

Excel

1. Let's define a table with 5 columns: Date (`column A`), Demand (`column B`), Forecast (`column C`), Level (`column D`), Trend (`column E`).
2. We will also indicate the learning rates: alpha and beta (`cells H1 and H2`). Don't forget – for the sake of clarity – to indicate that these represent alpha & beta.
3. We can initialize the first level as the first demand observation. The trend can be initialized as the difference between the first two demand observations. We won't give a value for the forecast on the first row as it makes no sense.
4. We can now type the formula for the forecast. This is rather easy, `cell C3` should be defined as `C3=D2+E2`. You can then copy-paste this formula until the end of the table.

---

[1] Did you know that – in the end – London wasn't buried under manure? It was saved, 20 years later, by motor vehicles.

Double Exponential Smoothing

	A	B	C	D	E	F	G	H
1	Date	Demand	Forecast	Level (a)	Trend (b)		Alpha:	30%
2	1	37		37	23		Beta:	40%
3	2	60	60					
4	3	85						
5	4	112						
6	5	132						
7	6	145						
8	7	179						
9	8	198						
10	9	212						
11	10	232						
12	11							
13	12							
14	13							

5. We will now create the level formula, we have to define D3 such that,

$$D3=\$H\$1*B3+(1-\$H\$1)*(D2+E2)$$

You can then copy-paste this formula until the end of the table.

6. We can now do the trend by defining E3 such that

$$E3=\$H\$2*(D3-D2)+(1-\$H\$2)*E2$$

You can also copy-paste this formula until one line after the end of the Demand column (until cell C12 in our case). You should have this result by now:

	A	B	C	D	E	F	G	H
1	Date	Demand	Forecast	Level (a)	Trend (b)		Alpha:	30%
2	1	37		37	23		Beta:	40%
3	2	60	60	60	23			
4	3	85	83	84	23			
5	4	112	107	108	24			
6	5	132	132	132	24			
7	6	145	156	153	23			
8	7	179	175	176	23			
9	8	198	199	199	23			
10	9	212	222	219	22			
11	10	232	240	238	21			
12	11		259					
13	12		279					
14	13		300					

7. Let's now extrapolate the forecast into the future. This is rather simple: in the cell C13, just type =C12+$E$11. You can then copy-

Do It Yourself

paste this formula further to see how the model predicts the demand.

Python

Double smoothing function

Just like for the simple model, we will define a function double_exp_smooth that takes a time series d as an input (it can be either a numpy array, a pandas DataFrame or a simple list) and returns a DataFrame that contains the historical demand, the forecast, the error, the level and the trend. The function can also take extra_periods as an optional input, which is the number of periods we want to forecast in the future. The last two optional inputs are the alpha and beta parameters.

```python
def double_exp_smooth(d,extra_periods=1,alpha=0.4,beta=0.4):

    d = np.array(d) # Transform the input into a numpy array
    cols = len(d) # Historical period length
    d = np.append(d,[np.nan]*extra_periods) # Append np.nan into the
        demand array to cover future periods

    # Creation of the level, trend and forecast arrays
    f,a,b = np.full((3,cols+extra_periods),np.nan)

    # Level & Trend initialization
    a[0] = d[0]
    b[0] = d[1] - d[0]

    # Create all the t+1 forecasts
    for t in range(1,cols):
        f[t] = a[t-1] + b[t-1]
        a[t] = alpha*d[t] + (1-alpha)*(a[t-1]+b[t-1])
        b[t] = beta*(a[t]-a[t-1]) + (1-beta)*b[t-1]

    # Forecast for all extra periods
    for t in range(cols,cols+extra_periods):
        f[t] = a[t-1] + b[t-1]
        a[t] = f[t]
        b[t] = b[t-1]

    df = pd.DataFrame.from_dict({"Demand":d,"Forecast":f,"Level":a,"Trend":b,"Error":d-f})

    return df
```

Note that we create the arrays for a,b & f in one instruction via

```
f,a,b = np.full((3,cols+extra_periods),np.nan)
```

The array generated by `np.full((3,cols+extra_periods),np.nan)` is actually unpacked by Python along its first axis and allocated to 3 variables (f,a,b in our case).

Playing with our function

Let's take back the same dummy demand time series as in chapter 3 and call our new function to forecast it.

```
import numpy as np
import pandas as pd
d=[28,19,18,13,19,16,19,18,13,16,16,11,18,15,13,15,13,11,13,10,12]
df = double_exp_smooth(d,extra_periods=4)
```

If we compute the accuracy KPI, we'll see that we get much worse results than what we obtained with our simple smoothing model (page 35).

```
MAE = df["Error"].abs().mean()
print("MAE:",MAE)
RMSE = np.sqrt((df["Error"]**2).mean())
print("RMSE:",RMSE)
```

```
MAE: 4.38
RMSE: 6.26
```

In order to understand what is happening, let's visualize our forecast.

```
df.index.name = "Periods"
df[["Demand","Forecast"]].plot(figsize=(8,3),title="Double Smoothing",ylim
    =(0,30),style=["-","--"])
```

As you can see on figure 5.3, the model overreacts to the initial trend.

Here are some ideas to improve it:

- Test other smoothing parameters for the trend and the level (we'll discuss this in chapter 6).
- Change the initialization method for the trend.
- Add a damped trend (we'll discuss it in chapter 7).

Do It Yourself

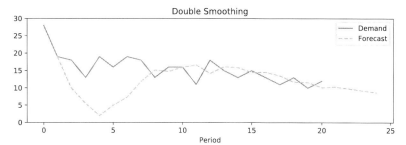

Figure 5.3: Example of double smoothing forecast

Chapter 6

Model Optimization

It is difficult to make predictions, especially about the future.
Author unknown.

Now that we have seen a couple of forecast models, we can discuss parameter optimization. Let's recap the models we have seen so far and their different parameters,

Moving Average n (chapter 1 page 3)
Simple exponential smoothing alpha (chapter 3 page 27)
Double exponential smoothing alpha, beta (chapter 5 page 41)

As we have seen on the double exponential smoothing case, a wrong parameter optimization will lead to catastrophic results. To optimize our models, we could of course manually search for the best parameter values. But remember that would be against our supply chain data science best practices: we need to automate our experiments in order to scale them. Thanks to our favorite tools – Excel and Python – we will be able to automatically look for the best parameter values. The idea is to set an objective (either RMSE or MAE[1]), automatically run through different parameter values and then select the one that gave the best results.

Excel

To optimize the parameters in Excel, we will use the Excel solver. If you have never used the Excel solver before, do not worry. It is rather easy.

---
[1]We discussed their strengths and limitations in chapter 2 (page 15).

Solver activation

The first step is to activate the solver in Excel. If you have a Windows machine with Excel 2010, 2013 or 2016, you can activate it via these steps,

1. Open Excel, go to File/Options/Add-ins,
2. click on the Manage drop-down menu, select Excel Add-ins and click on the Go... button just right to it.
3. On the add-ins box, click on the Solver Add-in check box and then click the Ok button to confirm your choice.
4. Let's now confirm that the solver is activated. In the Excel ribbon, go for the Data tab, there on the sub menu Analyze (normally on the far right) you should see the Solver button.

If you have another version of Excel or if you use a Mac, do not hesitate to google for help (search for "How to activate Excel Solver").

Forecast KPI

Let's take back the Excel sheet that we made for our double exponential smoothing implementation. We had a table that looked like this:

	A	B	C	D	E	F	G	H
1	Date	Demand	Forecast	Level (a)	Trend (b)		Alpha:	30%
2	1	37		37	23		Beta:	40%
3	2	60	60	60	23			
4	3	85	83	84	23			
5	4	112	107	108	24			
6	5	132	132	132	24			
7	6	145	156	153	23			
8	7	179	175	176	23			
9	8	198	199	199	23			
10	9	212	222	219	22			
11	10	232	240	238	21			
12	11		259					
13	12		279					
14	13		300					

Let's add some columns to calculate RMSE and MAE.

1. Create two new columns between columns E and F. One named "Absolute Error" (column F) and the second "Squared Error" (column G)

2. Calculate the absolute error in `cell F4` as `=abs(C4-B4)`, then the squared error in `cell G4` as `=F4^2`. We won't compute the forecast error for the first two demand observations (on `row 2:3`) as it simply doesn't make sense.
3. Copy-paste the formula in `cells F4` and `G4` until the end of the table. Don't go beyond the historical period: it makes no sense to calculate the error for future forecasts as there is no demand to compare it to!
4. Finally, add two new cells for RMSE and MAE (`cells J3` and `J4` respectively) and define them as follows:

$$J3 = SQRT(AVERAGE(G:G))$$
$$J4 = AVERAGE(F:F)$$

You should now have a table like the one below.

	A	B	C	D	E	F	G	H	I	J
1	Date	Demand	Forecast	Level (a)	Trend (b)	Absolute Error	Squared Error		Alpha:	30%
2	1	37		37	23				Beta:	40%
3	2	60	60	60	23				RMSE	6,3
4	3	85	83	84	23	2	4		MAE	5,1
5	4	112	107	108	24	5	25			
6	5	132	133	133	24	1	1			
7	6	145	157	153	22	12	136			
8	7	179	175	176	23	4	14			
9	8	198	199	199	23	1	1			
10	9	212	221	218	21	9	86			
11	10	232	239	237	20	7	54			
12	11		259							

Safety first Before going further with the solver, I would advise you to save your documents and close any other Excel document. The Excel solver will perform a lot of computations and it can take some time to run – especially on big files. Do not worry, our example will just take a couple of seconds to run, but we don't want Excel to crash with unsaved documents in case of an error.

Solver Optimization

We can now use the solver to find the best parameters. To do so, you need to access the `Data` menu in the Excel ribbon and then click on the `Solver` button in the `Analyze` submenu (normally on the far right of the screen). You will then have a menu such as shown on figure 6.1 (except yours will be empty).

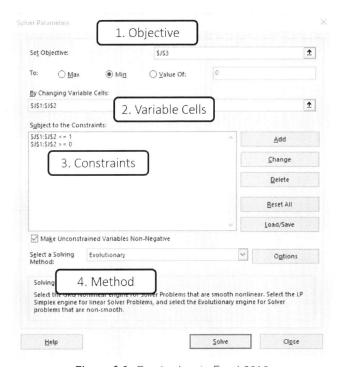

Figure 6.1: Excel solver in Excel 2016

You need to change 4 parameters:

1. Objective – In the Set Objective cell, you will need to indicate the cell you want to optimize. Typically, you want to optimize the model for the lowest MAE (cell J4) or RMSE (cell J3). Then, to tell Excel that you want to minimize the MAE/RMSE, you need to change the To: field to Min.

2. Variables – Now, we need to tell the solver what parameters it can play with. For this model, Excel can only play with alpha and beta. So we need to indicate cells $J$1:$J$2. Do not worry about the $ signs: you can input the cell range without them, as Excel will add them automatically.

3. Constraints – We now have to give some constraints to the solver. Typically for this model, we don't want alpha and beta to be above 1 or below 0. To add these constraints, click on the Add button on the right. You will then have a dialog box as shown on figure 6.2. You will need to input the cell you want to have a constraint on in the Cell Reference box. For our example, these will be the alpha and beta cells (J1 and J2). Then you indicate the constraint type ($\leq$ or

$\geq$) and the constraint.

Figure 6.2: Add a constraint

You will have to do this twice: once to indicate that alpha and beta should be below 1 and a second time to indicate that they should be above 0.

4. Method — You have to select the `Evolutionary` method in the list. The other methods won't work on this type of optimization problem (the explanation of these methods goes beyond the scope of this book).

Once this is done, click on the `solve` button and wait for Excel to optimize the parameter values. If everything goes fine, you will get values similar to figure 6.3. For an optimization of RMSE, Excel will choose alpha = 29% and beta = 0%.

	A	B	C	D	E	F	G	H	I	J
1	Date	Demand	Forecast	Level (a)	Trend (b)	Absolute Error	Squared Error		Alpha:	29%
2	1	37		37					Beta:	0%
3	2	60	60	60					RMSE	6,1
4	3	85	83	84			4		MAE	4,9
5	4	112	107	109			23			
6	5	132	134	133			3			
7	6	145	158	154			160			
8	7	179	175	176			18			
9	8	198	198	198			0			
10	9	212	220	218	20	8	65			
11	10	232	237	236	18	5	29			
12	11		255							

Figure 6.3: Optimization results

Python

Optimization function

In Python, we will use a simple method: we will test multiple values of alpha and beta for each model and select the one with the best outcome (based on any KPI we want). More specifically, we will loop through different alpha and beta values and save for each model (simple smoothing and double smoothing in this example) the parameter values, the model output and the KPI achieved (here MAE). At the end of all the trials, we will select the model which achieved the best KPI. In order to return the model that achieved the lowest error, we will have to use a new function: `np.argmin()`.

> `np.argmin()` returns the location of the minimum value in an array. Here is a simple example:

```
ar = np.array([1,2,3,4,-20])
np.argmin(ar)
Out: 4
```

Remember that, in Python, the location of the first element in an array is 0, so that the 5th element has location 4.

The function `np.argmax()` also exists. It returns the position of the highest element in an array.

```
def exp_smooth_opti(d,extra_periods=6):

    param = [] # contains all the different parameter sets
    KPI = [] # contains the results of each model
    outputs = [] # contains all the dataframes returned by the different
        models

    for alpha in [0.05,0.1,0.2,0.3,0.4,0.5,0.6]:

        df = simple_exp_smooth(d,extra_periods=extra_periods,alpha=alpha)
        param.append("Simple Smoothing, alpha: "+str(alpha))
        outputs.append(df)
        MAE = df["Error"].abs().mean()
        KPI.append(MAE)

        for beta in [0.05,0.1,0.2,0.3,0.4]:
```

Python

```
            df = double_exp_smooth(d,extra_periods=extra_periods,alpha=
                alpha,beta=beta)
            param.append("Double Smoothing, alpha: "+str(alpha)+", beta
                : "+str(beta))
            outputs.append(df)
            MAE = df["Error"].abs().mean()
            KPI.append(MAE)

    mini = np.argmin(KPI)
    print("Best solution found for",param[mini],"MAE of",round(KPI[mini
        ],2))

    return outputs[mini]
```

Playing with our function

Let's now run our function with our dummy demand dataset.

```
import numpy as np
import pandas as pd
d = [28,19,18,13,19,16,19,18,13,16,16,11,18,15,13,15,13,11,13,10,12]
df = exp_smooth_opti(d)
```

This is what we obtain.

```
Best solution found for Simple Smoothing, alpha: 0.4 MAE of 2.74
```

As usual, we can now plot the output.

```
df[["Demand","Forecast"]].plot(figsize=(8,3),title="Best model found",ylim
    =(0,30),style=["-","--"])
```

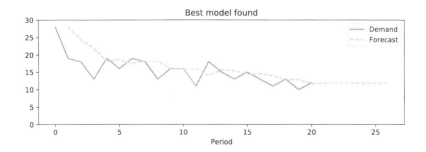

Chapter 7

Double Smoothing with Damped Trend

Idea

One of the limitations of the double smoothing model is the fact that the trend is assumed to go on forever. In 1985, Gardner and McKenzie proposed in their paper "Forecasting Trends in Time Series"[4] to add a new layer of intelligence to the double exponential model: a **damping factor**, **phi** (ϕ), that will exponentially reduce the trend over time. One could say that this new model **forgets** the trend over time. Or that the model remembers only a fraction (ϕ) of the previous estimated trend.

Practically, the trend (b) will be reduced by a factor ϕ at each period. In theory, ϕ will be between 0 and 1 – so that it can be seen as a % (like α and β). Nevertheless, in practice it is often between 0.7 and 1.

Model

We will take back the double exponential smoothing model and multiply all b_{t-1} occurrences by ϕ. Remember that $\phi \leq 1$, so that we forget a part of the previous trend. We then have,

$$a_t = \alpha d_t + (1-\alpha)(a_{t-1} + \phi b_{t-1})$$
$$b_t = \beta(a_t - a_{t-1}) + (1-\beta)\phi b_{t-1}$$

The forecast for the next period would then be,

$$f_{t+1} = a_t + b_t \phi$$

Or to be more general for a forecast made on period t for period $t + \lambda$,

$$f_{t+\lambda} = a_t + b_t \sum_{i=1}^{\lambda} \phi^i$$

Unfortunately, this generalization is not straightforward in Excel. Let's for example imagine you want to forecast period $t + 3$. You would have:

$$f_{t+3} = a_t + b_t\phi + b_t\phi^2 + b_t\phi^3$$

Note that if $\phi = 1$, then we are back to a normal double smoothing model, setting $\phi = 1$ basically means that the model won't forget the trend over time.

Insights

If we take back our example from the double exponential smoothing chapter, we obtain this graph.

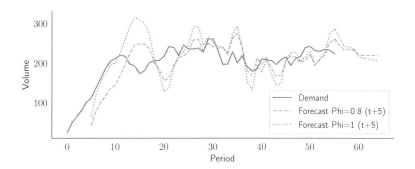

We have made two forecasts (both for $t + 5$): one with a damping factor of .8 and one without (i.e. $\phi = 1$). You can observe two things:

- The damping factor smoothes the extreme forecasts. This is quite helpful in many cases, but results in a poor forecast when the demand is growing with a steady trend (see the left part of the graph).

- The damping factor drastically reduces the impact of the trend for the future forecast. In the end, we are interested in the future forecast, so this aspect is the most important. With the damped trend, the model will forget the trend and the forecast will remain at a stable level. Whereas without damping, the model risks to be over-optimistic or pessimistic concerning the trend. See in the example how the forecast made without damping is assuming that the trend goes on forever. The forecast will eventually get negative.

Limitations

Thanks to the damping factor (ϕ), we solved the main limitation of the vanilla double smoothing model: the trend doesn't go on forever anymore. This damping factor might at first glance seems a simple idea, but it actually allows us to be much more accurate for mid and long-term forecasts.

Nevertheless, we still miss the ability for our model to recognize a seasonal pattern and apply it in the future. Many supply chains do face seasonality one way or the other, so we need our forecast models to be smart enough to fit these patterns. In order to do so, we will add a third layer of exponential smoothing in the following chapters.

Do It Yourself

Excel

Let's once again take back our Excel from the double exponential smoothing:

	A	B	C	D	E	F	G	H
1	Date	Demand	Forecast	Level (a)	Trend (b)		Alpha:	30%
2	1	37		37	23		Beta:	40%
3	2	60	60	60	23			
4	3	85	83	84	23			
5	4	112	107	108	24			
6	5	132	132	132	24			
7	6	145	156	153	23			
8	7	179	175	176	23			
9	8	198	199	199	23			
10	9	212	222	219	22			
11	10	232	240	238	21			
12	11		259					
13	12		279					
14	13		300					

From here you will need to

1. Add a new cell for the ϕ factor. We will use cell H3 (just below alpha & beta). Let's start with a value of 80% for ϕ.
2. Update the trend formula in E3 so that

    E3 = $H$2*(D3-D2)+(1-$H$2)*E2*$H$3

    Compared to the original formula, you only need to add the *$H$3 on the right. Once done, you can copy-paste it until the end of the table.
3. Now you can update the level formula in cell D3:

    D3 = $H$1*B3+(1-$H$1)*(D2+E2*$H$3)

    Just as for the trend, you only need to multiply E2 by $H$3 to update this formula. Once done, simply copy-paste this formula until the end of the table.
4. Let's now update the forecast formula in cell C2. We should now have,

    C2 = D2+E2*$H$3

    Again, you will need to copy-paste this formula until the end of the table.

You should now have this table:

	A	B	C	D	E	F	G	H
1	Date	Demand	Forecast	Level (a)	Trend (b)		Alpha:	30%
2	1	37	37	37	23		Beta:	40%
3	2	60	55	57	19		Phi:	80%
4	3	85	72	76	19			
5	4	112	91	97	20			
6	5	132	113	119	21			
7	6	145	135	138	20			
8	7	179	154	162	21			
9	8	198	179	185	22			
10	9	212	202	205	21			
11	10	232	222	225	21			
12	11		242					

Python

Damped double smoothing function

Just like the double exponential smoothing function, we define a new function double_exp_smooth_damped that takes a time series d as an input

Do It Yourself

and returns a `DataFrame` containing the historical demand, the forecast, the level, the trend and the error. The function can also take parameters `alpha` and `beta` as optional inputs.

```python
def double_exp_smooth_damped(d,extra_periods=1,alpha=0.4,beta=0.4,phi
    =0.9):

    d = np.array(d) # Transform the input into a numpy array
    cols = len(d) # Historical period length
    d = np.append(d,[np.nan]*extra_periods) # Append np.nan into the
        demand array to cover future periods

    # Creation of the level, trend and forecast arrays
    f,a,b = np.full((3,cols+extra_periods),np.nan)

    # Level & Trend initialization
    a[0] = d[0]
    b[0] = d[1] - d[0]

    # Create all the t+1 forecasts
    for t in range(1,cols):
        f[t] = a[t-1] + phi*b[t-1]
        a[t] = alpha*d[t] + (1-alpha)*(a[t-1]+phi*b[t-1])
        b[t] = beta*(a[t]-a[t-1]) + (1-beta)*phi*b[t-1]

    # Forecast for all extra periods
    for t in range(cols,cols+extra_periods):
        f[t] = a[t-1] + phi*b[t-1]
        a[t] = f[t]
        b[t] = phi*b[t-1]

    df = pd.DataFrame.from_dict({"Demand":d,"Forecast":f,"Level":a,"
        Trend":b,"Error":d-f})

    return df
```

Playing with our function

Let's test our new function on the same dummy demand time series as for the previous models.

```python
import numpy as np
import pandas as pd

```

```
4  d=[28,19,18,13,19,16,19,18,13,16,16,11,18,15,13,15,13,11,13,10,12]
5  df = double_exp_smooth_damped(d,extra_periods=4)
```

Let's take a look at the forecast accuracy:

```
1  MAE = df["Error"].abs().mean()
2  print("MAE:",MAE)
3  RMSE = np.sqrt((df["Error"]**2).mean())
4  print("RMSE:",RMSE)
```

```
1  MAE: 3.48
2  RMSE: 4.72
```

We already some better results than with the traditional double smoothing. You can of course optimize further the smoothing parameters (α, β & ϕ) thanks to the method described in chapter 6.

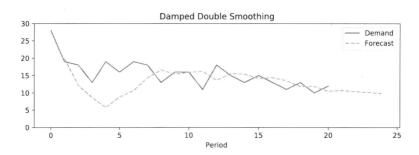

Chapter 8

Overfitting

We saw in chapter 4 the issue of underfitting a dataset. That is for a model not to be able to learn the patterns present in the training dataset. As we saw, underfitting is most likely due to the model not being smart enough to understand the training dataset and this could be solved by using a better (i.e. more complex) model.

On the other end of the spectrum, we have the risk of overfitting the data. If a model overfits the data, it means that it has recognized (or learned) patterns from the noise (i.e. randomness) of the training set. As it learns patterns from the noise, it will re-apply these patterns in the future on new data. **This will create an issue as the model will show (very) good results on the training dataset but will fail to make good predictions on the test set**. As we learn more complex models, underfitting will become less and less of an issue and overfitting will become the biggest risk.

Overfitting means that you learned patterns that worked **by chance** on the training set. And as, most likely, these patterns won't occur again on future data, you will make wrong predictions.

Actually, overfitting is the #1 enemy of many data scientists for another reason. Data scientists are always looking to make the best models with the highest accuracy. When a model achieves (very) good accuracy, it is then always tempting to think that this model is simply very good and call it a day. But careful analysis will reveal that the model is just overfitting the data. Overfitting can be seen as a mirage: one is tempted to think that there is an oasis in the middle of the desert. But actually it is just sand reflecting the sky. As we start to use machine learning (as of chapter

12), we will have to use more and more complex techniques to prevent our models from overfitting our datasets. Our battle against overfitting will reach a peak in chapter 18, when we discuss feature optimization...

Be careful with results on the training set.

Examples

Supply Chain Forecast

Let's imagine we have an item for which we want to use our optimization algorithm from chapter 6 to make a forecast. We have the historical demand from periods 0 to 20 and we run our algorithm on these periods. If we obtain an RMSE of 10%, can we assume this accuracy to be obtained for future predictions as well? No.

As you can see below, based on the optimization until period 20, we choose a specific parameter set (e.g. $\alpha = 0.7$, $\beta = 1$ & $\phi = 0.9$) and keep applying this specific set over time for the future forecast.

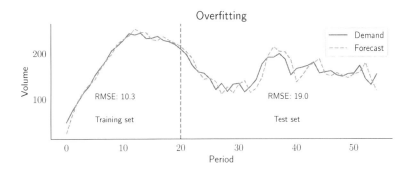

Unfortunately, around the 30th period, we get a decrease in accuracy as the forecast is overreacting to changes in the trend. In our example, the RMSE is nearly doubled from period 20 onwards compared to periods 0 to 20. This is overfitting.

Business world

In his book "The Signal and the Noise" [12], Nate Silver (also author of the blog fivethirtyeight.com) gives a perfect example of overfitting in stock market predictions.

Examples

> *A once-famous "leading indicator" of economic performance, for instance, was the winner of the Super Bowl. From Super Bowl I in 1967 through Super Bowl XXXI in 1997, the stock market gained an average of 14 percent for the rest of the year when a team from the original National Football League (NFL) won the game. But it fell by almost 10 percent when a team from the original American Football League (AFL) won instead. Through 1997, this indicator had correctly "predicted" the direction of the stock market in twenty-eight of thirty-one years. A standard test of statistical significance, if taken literally, would have implied that there was only about a 1-in-4,700,000 possibility that the relationship had emerged from chance alone. Whereas of course, there was no relationship at all between the stock market and sport events.*

The same effect happens regularly when political elections come closer. One can then often hear in the press that *"someone tested 100+ variables to predict who would win, and they found a perfect model for the last 10 elections"*. That is a perfect example of overfitting. If you look at 100 variables, you will – for sure – find that at least one of them matches whatever output you want to predict.

The website www.tylervigen.com made a specialty of finding these **random** strange relationships where you find a perfect statistical match. You can see on figure 8.1 the correlation between movies with Nicolas Cage and people who drowned in pools.

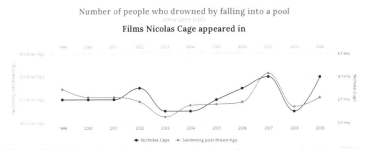

Figure 8.1: Example of spurious correlations from www.tylervigen.com

Causes & Solutions

So how do we protect ourselves from the overfitting trap?

Use less explanatory variables The more explanatory variables the model has, the more possibilities it will have to recognize patterns in the noise. This will become a bigger problem with the machine learning models we will see in the second part of the book. But it can happen as well with exponential smoothing models. We will see in chapters 9 and 11 two seasonal models that might recognize (and extrapolate) seasonality where there is none. Do not use a too complex model to fit a simple demand pattern.

Use more data More data will reduce the probability of seeing fake patterns.

Don't fit on the test set You should never use your test set to select a model or to train your model. It should only be used to get a final idea of the accuracy you can expect.

Validate on the test set You should only validate a model if it performs against the test dataset. A model that only performs well on a training dataset can't be trusted.

Chapter 9

Triple Exponential Smoothing

Idea

With the first two exponential smoothing models we saw, we learned how to identify the level and the trend of a time series and used these pieces of information to populate our forecast. After that, we added an extra layer of intelligence to the trend by allowing the model to forget it over time.

Unfortunately, the simple and double exponential smoothing models do not recognize seasonal patterns and therefore cannot extrapolate any seasonal behaviour in the future. Seasonal products – with high and low seasons – are common for many supply chains across the globe as seasonality can be caused by many different factors. This limitation is thus a real problem for our model.

In order for our model to learn a seasonal pattern, we will add a third layer of exponential smoothing. The idea is that the model will learn multiplicative **seasonal factors** that will be applied to each period inside a full seasonal cycle. As for the trend (β) and the level (α), the seasonal factors will be learned via an exponential weighting method with a new specific learning rate: **gamma** (γ).

Multiplicative seasonal factors mean, for example, that the model will know that the demand is increased by 20% in January (compared to the

yearly average) but reduced by 30% in February.
We will discuss the case of additive seasonality in chapter 11.

Model

The main idea is that now the forecast is composed of the level (a) plus the (damped) trend (b) **multiplied by** the seasonal factor (s).

$$f_t = (a_{t-1} + \phi b_{t-1})s_{t-p}$$

Pay attention, we need to use the seasonal factors that were calculated the previous season: s_{t-p} where p is the season length (p for periodicity)[1]. The different seasonal factors (s) can be seen as **percentages** to be applied to the level in order to obtain the forecast. For example, for a monthly forecast, the statement *"We sell 20% more in January"* would be translated as $s_{january} = 120\%$.

Component updates

We calculate the different demand components as such:

$$a_t = \alpha \frac{d_t}{s_{t-p}} \quad +(1-\alpha)(a_{t-1} + \phi b_{t-1})$$
$$b_t = \beta(a_t - a_{t-1}) \quad +(1-\beta)\phi b_{t-1}$$
$$s_t = \gamma \frac{d_t}{a_t} \quad +(1-\gamma)s_{t-p}$$

Level & Trend Let's first discuss the level (a) and the trend (b). They are both deseasonalized. See how a is updated based on the most recent demand observation d_t divided by the seasonality s_{t-p}. As the trend is the difference between two consecutive levels, it is also deseasonalized.

Seasonal factors The seasonal factor s_t is then estimated based on its most recent observation (the demand divided by the level) and its previous estimation (just like a and b). Parameter γ will also determine how much weight is given to the most recent observation compared to the previous estimation. Just like α and β, γ is also theoretically between 0 and 1 (so that it can be seen as a % value) but in practice it is usually rather low (< 0.3). Business wise, it is rather exceptional to assume that the seasonality could drastically change from one year to another. With a high γ, you might face overfitting.

---

[1] Typically, the periodicity will be 12 for yearly cycles.

Model

Seasonal factors scaling

On average, the seasonal factors must be equal to 1 (or 100% if you interpret them as percentages). This is important as the seasonal factors determine how the forecast is **allocated** within a full seasonal cycle. But they do not impact the total demand of a full seasonal cycle, as on average we will allocate 100% to each period.

You can interpret this by saying that if we sell 20% more than usual in January, we must be selling 20% less than usual in another month.

If we translate this in mathematical language, we have:

$$\frac{\sum_{cycle} s}{p} = 1 \leftrightarrow \sum_{cycle} s = p$$

Where p is the season length. Which means that on average the seasonal factors are 1 (or 100%) and their sum over the full seasonal cycle should be p (i.e. the number of periods inside a seasonal cycle). This implies that the level is on the same scale as the demand and the forecast, as it is multiplied on average[1] by 1.

Future forecast

We can generalize the forecast for period $t+1$ to a forecast for period $t+\lambda$

$$f_{t+\lambda} = \left(a_t + b_t \sum_{i=1}^{i} \phi^\lambda\right) s_{t-p+\lambda}$$

If we don't use a damping factor, we have this simpler equation:

$$f_{t+\lambda} = (a_t + \lambda b_t) s_{t-p+\lambda}$$

Component initialization

There are some discussions in the literature on how to initialize the seasonal factors for exponential smoothing algorithms. Let's just use a simple method here: we will initialize the seasonal factors based on the historical demand.

We will do this in multiple steps.

---

[1] In practice – in order to simplify the seasonal factors update procedure – you can allow the seasonal factors to slightly drift away from p over time.

1. **Compute the historical season averages.**
   You can see on table 9.1 an example of quarterly seasonal demand over 5 years. We have computed the average demand per quarter on the last column. Unfortunately, we cannot use these historical

	Y1	Y2	Y3	Y4	Y5	Mean
Q1	14	18	16	18	17	16.6
Q2	10	8	9	11	9	9.4
Q3	6	4	5	4	5	4.8
Q4	2	1	3	2	1	1.8

   Table 9.1: Example of seasonal demand

   season averages as seasonal factors for our model as **they are not scaled**. Remember: the sum of the seasonal factors should be equal to p (4 in our example), so that we can **interpret them as percentages**.

2. **Scale the historical season averages.**
   We will scale our historical averages so that their sum will be equal to 4. In order to do this, we will **divide** our historical season averages by their own mean (8.15).

	Y1	Y2	Y3	Y4	Y5	Mean	Factors
Q1	14	18	16	18	17	16.6	2.04
Q2	10	8	9	11	9	9.4	1.15
Q3	6	4	5	4	5	4.8	0.59
Q4	2	1	3	2	1	1.8	0.22
Mean						8.15	1.00

3. We now obtain a scaled set of seasonal factors: 2.04, 1.15, 0.59 & 0.22. You can interpret them as saying: *"We sell 104% extra units in Q1, and we sell +15% in Q2 but -41% in Q3 and -78% in Q4"*. As you can see, these seasonal factors are now properly scaled, as their sum is equal to the periodicity (4) and their average is 1. This is perfect, as it means that the level (a) will be, on average, multiplied by 1 to obtain a forecast, so that they are both on the same scale.

Note that if you have an important trend in the historical demand, you might face an issue and you should potentially first remove the trend in your data before computing the seasonal factors.

Other methods

We also love to experiment, so you could also try your own methods. Here are some ideas:

- Initialize the seasonal factors as simply the first historical season.
- Use common seasonal factors for similar products (that could help against overfitting).
- Apply any seasonal factors that you think are correct based on your business experience.

There is no strictly better method. In order to find the most appropriate one for your dataset, you will have to use a scientific approach: test different methods and see which one gives the best result. In any case, do not forget to scale the seasonal factors so that their sum is equal to p, so that they can be interpreted as percentages.

Insights

First example

Let's plot an example based on dummy data to see how this works in practice:

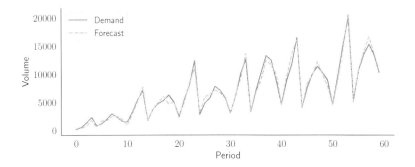

We have used $\alpha = 0.8$, $\beta = 0.1$ and $\gamma = 0.4$. We see on this dummy dataset how close the forecast at $t+1$ is to the demand, even though the demand is drastically changing over time.

Let's now plot the seasonal factors to see how they change over time.

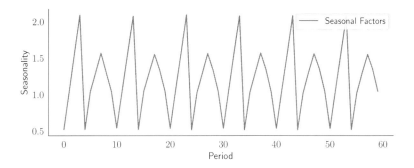

Actually, it seems that the seasonal factors do not change so much over time. Let's see then how the trend evolves.

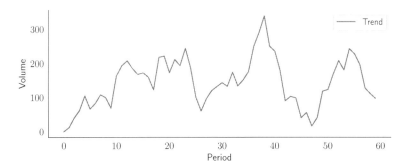

The model behaves as expected: the seasonality doesn't vary much over time. Instead, it is the level and the trend that evolve more over time. This is perfect as it makes little sense to expect the seasonality of a product to change much over time.

Intermittent products

One of the issues of a multiplicative seasonality appears when you deal with low demand: the model might overreact to level changes if the level is too close to 0. Remember that the seasonality is defined as such:

$$s_t = \gamma \frac{d_t}{a_t} + (1-\gamma)s_{t-p}$$

Insights

A small absolute demand variation (from one piece to five pieces) can result in a huge difference of seasonality (100% to 500%). Let's take an example with the following quarterly demand:

	Y1	Y2	Y3	Y4	Y5	Y6
Q1	14	18	16	18	17	?
Q2	10	8	9	11	9	?
Q3	6	4	5	4	5	?
Q4	2	1	3	2	1	?

Most likely, you saw that in Q1 we can expect something between 16 and 18, then a demand around 10 pieces for Q2, 5 pieces for Q3 and 2 pieces for Q4. Let's see how our model handles this.

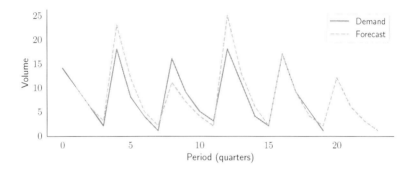

Here, we have used a model with $\alpha = 0.4$, $\beta = 0.4$, $\phi = 0.9$ and $\gamma = 0.3$. We see that even though the demand is very stable, the forecast seems too low for Y6. Actually, if you look at the seasonal factors, they are pretty stable at around $[2.0, 1.1, 0.6, 0.2]$. The error lies in how the level is massively impacted by Q4 (see periods 15–20 on figure 9.1).

We will come back to this example later (in chapter 11) with our next model: the additive trend.

Undefined models A worst case can even happen if any of the initial seasonal parameters is estimated to be 0. Remember that the level estimation is made by dividing the current demand observation by a seasonal factor. If any of the seasonal factors is 0, this level estimation will fail as the model will have to do a division by 0.

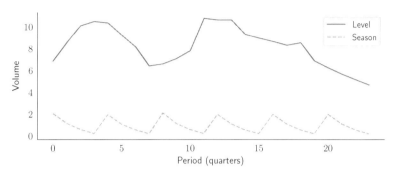

Figure 9.1: Level & seasonality evolution

Limitations

This new triple exponential smoothing is a fantastic model as we can now deal with seasonal products. Unfortunately, as discussed, the multiplicative part of the model might result in (mathematical) errors if the demand level or the seasonality factors are too close to 0. This means that this model is unfortunately not suited for all products. To solve this, we will work next on a model with an additive seasonality.

Do It Yourself

Excel

As an Excel model is more complicated for a triple exponential smoothing, we will start from scratch on a simple example for a quarterly demand. We won't implement a damped trend to focus on the seasonal part. We will work on the demand dataset we used in the previous examples:

	Y1	Y2	Y3	Y4	Y5
Q1	14	18	16	18	17
Q2	10	8	9	11	9
Q3	6	4	5	4	5
Q4	2	1	3	2	1

Let's open a new Excel sheet to create our model.

1. We will start by creating the table layout for our data by creating multiple columns:

    Date in column A

Do It Yourself

Demand in column B
Forecast in column C
Level in column D
Trend in column E
Seasonality in column F

2. Let's add next to this the cells with our different parameters:

   Alpha in cell I1
   Beta in cell I2
   Gamma in cell I3

   with their respective names in column H. You should now have an Excel sheet that looks like this:

	A	B	C	D	E	F	G	H	I
1	Date	Demand	Forecast	Level (a)	Trend (b)	Season (s)		Alpha:	80%
2	1	14						Beta:	10%
3	2	10						Gamma:	40%
4	3	6							
5	4	2							
6	5	18							
7	6	8							
8	7	4							
9	8	1							

3. Once this is done, we need to initialize our model. We have to do this for the level, the trend and the seasonality. Let's keep it simple for this example.

   Seasonality For the first year it is initialized as [2.0; 1.2; 0.6; 0.2] in cells F2:F5

   Level We initialize the level on $t = 1$ as

   $$a_{t=1} = \frac{D_{t=1}}{S_{t=1}}$$

   which means that in cell D2 we type =B2/F2

   Trend We initialize the trend on $t = 1$ as

   $$b_{t=1} = \frac{D_{t=2}}{S_{t=2}} - \frac{D_{t=1}}{S_{t=1}}$$

   which means that in cell D2 we type =B3/F3-B2/F2

4. We can now start to do our forecast during the first year.

   Level As of the 2nd quarter, we have

   $$a_t = \alpha \frac{d_t}{s_t} + (1-\alpha)(a_{t-1} + b_{t-1})$$

Note that we use the initial seasonal factors to populate the forecast during the first year. Which means that we will use the formula below for `cell D3`

```
D3 = $I$1*B3/F3+(1-$I$1)*(D2+E2)
```

You can then copy-paste it until `cell D4`.

Trend We use this formula

$$b_t = \beta(a_t - a_{t-1}) + (1-\beta)b_{t-1}$$

We will implement this formula in `cell F3`

```
E3 = $I$2*(D3-D2)+(1-$I$2)*E2
```

You can copy-paste this until the end of the table as it is independent from the seasonal factors.

5. We can now do the forecast from the second year until the end of the historical period.

    Level As of the 5th quarter, we should use the previous-year seasonal factor.

    $$a_t = \alpha \frac{d_t}{s_{t-p}} + (1-\alpha)(a_{t-1} + b_{t-1})$$

    You then need to input this formula in `cell D6`

    ```
    D6 = $I$1*B6/F2+(1-$I$1)*(D5+E5)
    ```

    You can then copy-paste it until the end of the table.

    Trend We use the same formula as for the first period.

    Season We need to update the seasonal factors based on:

    $$s_t = \gamma \frac{d_t}{a_t} + (1-\gamma)s_{t-p}$$

    We will input in `cell F6`

    ```
    F6 = $I$3*(B6/D6)+(1-$I$3)*F2
    ```

    and copy-paste it until the end of the table.

6. We can now populate the future forecast that will be based on the latest seasonality factors.

    Level We will update the level at each new period by the trend. You can type `=D21+E21` in `cell D22`.

Do It Yourself

Trend The trend will remain constant (remember we don't use a damped trend here for the sake of simplicity). So that you can type =E21 in `cell E22`.

Season We will simply copy the latest seasonal factors and extrapolate them. You can simply input =F18 in `cell F22`.

Once this is done, you can copy-paste the `cells D22:F22` downwards to get your future forecast!

7. We now have to define our forecast. We defined it as

$$f_t = (a_{t-1} + b_{t-1})s_{t-p-1}$$

Let's start by the first year where we need to use the current seasonal factors. In `cell C3`, you can type (D2+E2)*F2 and copy-paste it until `cell C5`. You can then define C6 as =(D5+E5)*F2 and copy-paste this until the end of the table.

	A	B	C	D	E	F	G	H	I
1	Date	Demand	Forecast	Level (a)	Trend (b)	Season (s)		Alpha:	80%
2	1	14		7,0	1,3	2,00		Beta:	10%
3	2	10	10	8,3	1,3	1,20		Gamma:	40%
4	3	6	6	9,9	1,4	0,60			
5	4	2	2	10,3	1,3	0,20			
6	5	18	23	9,5	1,1	1,96			
7	6	8	12	7,4	0,7	1,15			
8	7	4	5	7,0	0,6	0,59			
9	8	1	1	5,5	0,4	0,19			
10	9	16	12	7,7	0,6	2,00			
11	10	9	10	7,9	0,6	1,14			
12	11	5	5	8,5	0,6	0,59			
13	12	3	2	14,3	1,1	0,20			
14	13	18	29	10,3	0,6	1,90			
15	14	11	12	9,9	0,5	1,13			
16	15	4	6	7,5	0,2	0,57			
17	16	2	2	9,6	0,4	0,20			
18	17	17	19	9,1	0,3	1,89			
19	18	9	11	8,2	0,2	1,12			
20	19	5	5	8,7	0,2	0,57			
21	20	1	2	5,7	-0,1	0,19			
22	21		11	5,6	-0,1	1,89			
23	22		6	5,5	-0,1	1,12			
24	23		3	5,4	-0,1	0,57			
25	24		1	5,3	-0,1	0,19			
26									

As you can see, we are starting to reach a point where Excel does not seem to be the most appropriate tool anymore. Our Python functions will be much easier to implement, correct and update.

Python

Seasonal factors initialization

Let's first create a function to compute our (multiplicative) seasonal factors. In the future, if you want to play with the initialization method (maybe based on the different ideas of page 73), this will make your life easier.

```
def seasonal_factors_mul(s,d,slen,cols):
    for i in range(slen):
        idx = [x for x in range(cols) if x%slen==i] # Compute indices that
            correspond to this season
        s[i] = np.mean(d[idx]) # Compute season average
    s /= np.mean(s[:slen]) # Scale season factors (sum of factors = slen)
    return s
```

In the code above, we use the % operator which is the modulus operator in Python: it divides the left-hand value by the right-hand value and returns the remainder (e.g. 12%5 = 2).

Triple smoothing

As usual, we will create a function triple_exp_smooth_mul that will take a time series d and the season length slen as inputs. The function will also take as optional inputs the different smoothing parameters (alpha, beta, gamma & phi) and extra_periods (the number of extra periods we want to forecast in the future). The function will return a pandas DataFrame that contains the demand, forecast, level, trend, seasonal factors and the error.

```
def triple_exp_smooth_mul(d,slen=12,extra_periods=1,alpha=0.4,beta=0.4,
    phi=0.9,gamma=0.3):

    d = np.array(d) # Transform the input into a numpy array
    cols = len(d) # Historical period length
    d = np.append(d,[np.nan]*extra_periods) # Append np.nan into the
        demand array to cover future periods

    # components initialization
    f,a,b,s = np.full((4,cols+extra_periods),np.nan)
    s = seasonal_factors_mul(s,d,slen,cols)

    # Level & Trend initialization
```

Do It Yourself

```
        a[0] = d[0]/s[0]
        b[0] = d[1]/s[1] − d[0]/s[0]

        # Create the forecast for the first season
        for t in range(1,slen):
            f[t] = (a[t−1] + phi*b[t−1])*s[t]
            a[t] = alpha*d[t]/s[t] + (1−alpha)*(a[t−1]+phi*b[t−1])
            b[t] = beta*(a[t]−a[t−1]) + (1−beta)*phi*b[t−1]

        # Create all the t+1 forecasts
        for t in range(slen,cols):
            f[t] = (a[t−1] + phi*b[t−1])*s[t−slen]
            a[t] = alpha*d[t]/s[t−slen] + (1−alpha)*(a[t−1]+phi*b[t−1])
            b[t] = beta*(a[t]−a[t−1]) + (1−beta)*phi*b[t−1]
            s[t] = gamma*d[t]/a[t] + (1−gamma)*s[t−slen]

        # Forecast for all extra periods
        for t in range(cols,cols+extra_periods):
            f[t] = (a[t−1] + phi*b[t−1])*s[t−slen]
            a[t] = f[t]/s[t−slen]
            b[t] = phi*b[t−1]
            s[t] = s[t−slen]

        df = pd.DataFrame.from_dict({"Demand":d,"Forecast":f,"Level":a,
             "Trend":b,"Season":s,"Error":d−f})

        return df
```

You can then call this function to obtain a `DataFrame` with all the different components.

```
import numpy as np
import pandas as pd
d = [14,10,6,2,18,8,4,1,16,9,5,3,18,11,4,2,17,9,5,1]
df = triple_exp_smooth_mul(d)
```

Thanks to this `DataFrame`, we can compute the different forecast KPIs.

```
MAE = df["Error"].abs().mean() / df.loc[1:,"Demand"].mean()
print("MAE:",round(MAE,3)*100,"%")
RMSE = np.sqrt((df["Error"]**2).mean()) / df.loc[1:,"Demand"].mean()
print("RMSE:",round(RMSE,3)*100,"%")
```

This is what we obtain:

```
1  MAE: 8.6 %
2  RMSE: 12.1 %
```

Note that we divided MAE and RMSE by the average demand in order to express these two KPIs in percentages.

We could have computed the demand mean by simply typing `df.Demand.mean()` but we prefer to exclude the first demand observation from this mean as the forecast of the first period is undefined. We then compare apples to apples.

Visualization

We can use the method `.plot()` on our `DataFrame` to plot our time series and its components. Nevertheless, such a graph would be messy due to the amount of components and their different scales (see figure 9.2).

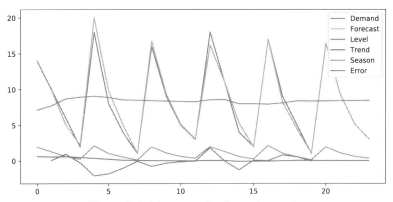

Figure 9.2: Messy graph of our time series

To overcome this, we have two solutions: we can plot our time series and its components

- with one subplot per component thanks to the command (see figure 9.3):

```
1  df.plot(subplots=True)
```

- with different y-axes/scales thanks to the command (see figure 9.4):

Do It Yourself

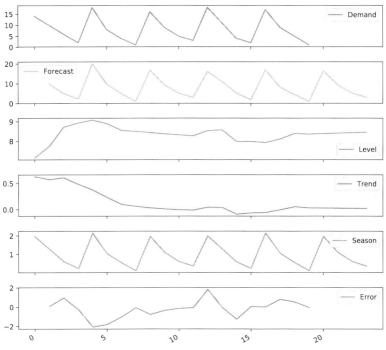

Figure 9.3: Subplots

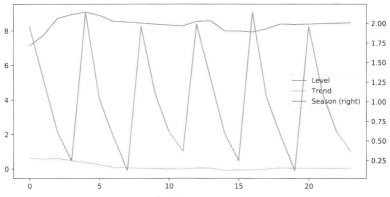

Figure 9.4: Plot with two axes

Chapter 10

Outliers

> *I shall not today attempt further to define this kind of material (...), and perhaps I could never succeed in intelligibly doing so. But I know it when I see it.*
> Potter Stewart

In 1964, Potter Stewart was a United States Supreme Court Justice. He wasn't discussing outliers but whether the movie *The Lovers* was or wasn't obscene.

As you work on forecast with the different models we saw – and the following models we will see later – you will notice that your dataset will have outliers. And even though *I know it when I see it* might be the only practical definition, these outliers pose a real threat to supply chains. These high (or low) points will result in over-reactions in your forecast or in your safety stocks, ultimately resulting in (at best) manual corrections or (at worst) dead stocks, losses and a nasty bullwhip effect. Actually, when you look at blogs, books, articles or software on forecast, the question of outlier detection is often eluded. This is a pity. **Outlier detection is serious business**.

These outliers pop out all the time in modern supply chains. They are mostly due to two main reasons:

Mistakes & errors These are obvious outliers. If you spot such kind of errors or encoding mistakes, it calls for process improvement in order to prevent these from happening again.

Exceptional demand Even though some demand observations are real, it does not mean they are not *exceptional* and shouldn't be cleaned or smoothed. This kind of exceptional sales are actually not so uncommon in supply chains. Think about promotions, marketing, strange customer behaviours or destocking. Typically, you might not want to take into account for your forecast the exceptional -80% sales you did last year to get rid of an old nearly-obsolete inventory.

If you can spot outliers and smooth them out, you will make a better forecast. I have seen numerous examples where the forecast error was reduced by a couple of percents just thanks to outlier cleaning. Actually, the bigger the dataset, the more important it is to *automate* this detection and cleaning. Let's see how we can do this.

In the following pages, we will discuss three and a half ideas to spot these outliers and put them back to a reasonable level.

Idea #1 - Winsorization

As we said, an outlier is an exceptionally high or low value. Based on this simple definition, a first idea to detect outliers would be to simply cut down the top x highest and lowest points of the dataset. Let's see how this would work on the two (dummy) datasets on tables 10.1 and 10.2.

Month	M1	M2	M3	M4	M5	M6	M7	M8	M9	M10	M11	M12
Y1	17	12	7	5	4	9	13	14	11	11	10	12
Y2	6	11	14	15	8	12	14	14	11	10	7	15
Y3	9	8	5	12	10	8	9	10	8	16	8	10

Table 10.1: Simple demand history

Month	M1	M2	M3	M4	M5	M6	M7	M8	M9	M10	M11	M12
Y1	17	12	7	5	4	9	13	14	11	11	10	12
Y2	6	11	14	15	8	12	100	14	11	10	7	15
Y3	9	8	5	12	10	8	9	10	8	16	8	10

Table 10.2: Simple demand history with outlier

This first technique will simply decrease the top/down x% values of our historical demand down to the limit of the xth **percentile**.

> **the xth percentile** is a value below which x% of the observations in a group will fall. For example, 99% of the demand observations for a product will be lower than its 99th percentile.

Idea #1 - Winsorization

This technique of simply shrinking the demand down to a certain percentile is called **winsorization**. The name comes from Charles P. Winsor, a statistician from the first half of the XXth century.

If we look at the 1st and 99th percentile on our two dummy datasets (10.1 and 10.2), this is what we obtain:

Dataset	Lower limit	Higher limit
#1	4.4	16.6
#2	4.4	70.9

Table 10.3: Outlier detection with winsorization

Table 10.3 tells us that in both datasets all the low values would be increased up to 4.3. You can see on figure 10.1 that this cuts a part of our dataset. The high values would be decreased down to 16.7 on the dataset without outliers (figure 10.1) and down to 70.9 for the dataset with an outlier (figure 10.2).

You might have noticed that the winsorization didn't give us round results such as 4 or 5, but instead we got this 4.3. Actually, as we don't have an exact value that cuts the dataset by 99%, we do a linear approximation based on the two closest values. This is how we got these numbers instead of round numbers.

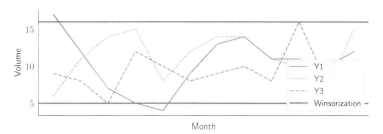

Figure 10.1: Winsorization on simple dataset

So, are we happy with this technique? No we're not.

- We have spotted fake outliers on a dataset without outliers.
- On the dataset with outliers, we haven't sufficiently reduced the outlier (it went from 100 to 70.9).

Of course, one could simply propose to decrease the higher limit of the winsorization from 99% to 95% to further reduce the outlier on dataset

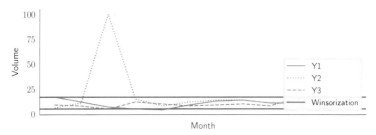

Figure 10.2: Winsorization on an extreme dataset

#2, but unfortunately this would also have an effect on dataset #1. This is not a good solution. One could also propose to remove this lower limit so that we don't increase our demand to 4.4. But, what if we have periods with missing demand? Shouldn't we clean these as well if any?

Do It Yourself

Excel you can easily get the different percentiles of a range of cells in Excel by using the formula =PERCENTILE.INC(range,limit). Of course you'll have to use this formula once for the upper limit (with a value around 0.95 - 0.99) and once for the lower limit (with a value around 0.01 - 0.05).

Python We can easily winsorize our dataset in Python thanks to NumPy. We can compute the different percentiles of an array thanks to the np.percentile(array,percentile) function.

```
import numpy as np
higher_limit = np.percentile(array, 99)
lower_limit = np.percentile(array, 1)
```

Note that the percentile function takes a percentile expressed as a value between 0 and 100 and not a ratio (i.e. a value between 0 and 1) like in Excel.

We can then simply cut the array to these lower and higher limits thanks to the function np.clip(array,min,max):

```
array = np.clip(array,a_min=lower_limit,a_max=higher_limit)
```

Idea #2 Standard deviation

As we just saw, winsorization wasn't the perfect way to exclude outliers as it would take out high and low values of a dataset even if they weren't exceptional per see.

Another approach would be to look at the demand variation around the historical average and exclude the values that are *exceptionally* far from this average.

Let's define the demand standard deviation as σ:

$$\sigma = \sqrt{\frac{\sum(demand - average)^2}{n}}$$

where *n* is the amount of demand observations we have.

If we assume that our data is normally distributed around the historical mean[1], **we can compute the probability for the demand to be between two thresholds**. These two thresholds will be centered on the demand average (μ) with a spread of *x* times the standard deviation (σ) in both directions. The more chaotic the demand (i.e. σ is big), the wider the thresholds.

Min threshold	<	Probability	<	Max threshold
$\mu - 1.28\sigma$	<	95%	<	$\mu + 1.28\sigma$
$\mu - 2.33\sigma$	<	98%	<	$\mu + 2.33\sigma$
$\mu - 2.58\sigma$	<	99%	<	$\mu + 2.58\sigma$

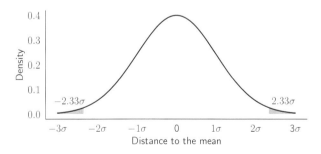

Figure 10.3: Normal curve excluding top & bottom 1% of values

For example, we have a 98% probability to be in the **range**: demand average ± 2.33 times the standard deviation (as in figure 10.3). So that

---
[1] the exact mathematics involved here are beyond the scope of the book, and unfortunately more often than not the assumption of normality is not strictly respected.

if we wanted to remove the top 1% of both high and low values, we would restrict the demand to $\mu \pm 2.33\sigma$.

Note that this means we have a 99% probability to be **lower** than $\mu + 2.33\sigma$. And a 99% probability to be **higher** than $\mu - 2.33\sigma$.

If we applied this to our example datasets (see tables 10.1 and 10.2), we would get these limits:

Dataset	Lower limit	Higher limit
#1	3.0	17.8
#2	-22.2	47.9

Table 10.4: Outlier detection based on standard deviation

Let's see how these new *normal* limits behave compared to the winsorization limits.

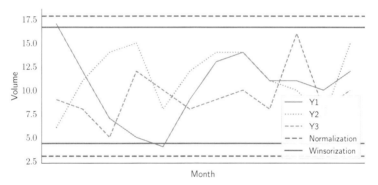

Figure 10.4: Simple dataset

This is already much better than the results we got with winsorization:

- On the dataset without outliers (see figure 10.4), we don't change any demand observation (perfect! – just as we want).
- On the dataset with an outlier, we don't change the low-demand points but only the actual outlier (see figure 10.5).

Still, even though we reduce the outlier to a more manageable amount (47.9) than with the winsorization (70.9), it might not be enough yet.

So, are we happy now? Not quite yet. As you might remember, we assumed the error to be around the historical mean. This is fine for a product with a flat demand, but the actual limitation will arise when you

Idea #2 Standard deviation

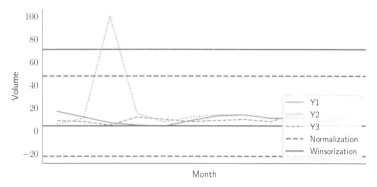

Figure 10.5: Extreme dataset

have a product with a trend or a seasonality. For example, on table 10.5, the highest (or lowest) points are no longer the outliers you want to remove.

Month	M1	M2	M3	M4	M5	M6	M7	M8	M9	M10	M11	M12
Y1	11	24	15	11	9	11	8	8	7	7	7	4
Y2	18	22	14	20	7	9	7	3	8	6	<u>19</u>	3
Y3	17	21	22	12	11	12	12	8	8	6	3	4

Table 10.5: Seasonal demand with outlier

You can see how winsorization and normalization work on this seasonal demand on figure 10.6. It simply doesn't make sense: both techniques flag the season peaks as outliers and they skip the *real* outlier which is Y2 M11.

We will solve this with our next technique.

Do It Yourself

Excel You can compute the standard deviation of a range of cells thanks to the formula =STDEV.P(range). As always, you can compute the mean thanks to =AVERAGE(range). Once you have these two, you can compute the higher and lower limits thanks to =NORM.INV(percentile, mean, stdev). Typically, you will want the high percentile to be around 0.99 and the low one around 0.01.

Python You can calculate the standard deviation via np.std(array) for an array-like (e.g. a list, a DataFrame etc.) or for a DataFrame directly via the method .std(). So that if you have a DataFrame df you can simply type:

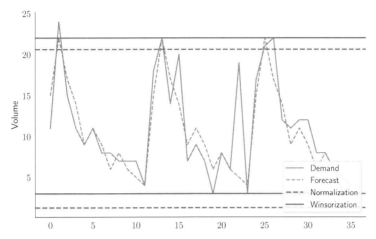

Figure 10.6: Winsorization & Normalization on seasonal dataset

```
m = df.mean()
s = df.std()
```

We will then once again use the SciPy library to compute the normal probabilities. We'll then use the .clip method on our DataFrame to cap it to our limits (see line 8).

```
from scipy.stats import norm

#Print the probabilities of each demand observation
print(norm.cdf(df.values, m, s).round(2))

limit_high = norm.ppf(0.99,m,s)
limit_low = norm.ppf(0.01,m,s)
df = df.clip(lower=limit_low, upper=limit_high)
```

Idea #3 Error standard deviation

The second idea we had to flag outliers was to compare each observation against the mean of the demand. We saw that it didn't make sense if we had a trend or a seasonality as the difference between an observation and the historical mean wasn't relevant.

Idea #3 Error standard deviation

Well, let's go back to the definition of an outlier: *an outlier is a value that you didn't expect*[1]. That is to say that an outlier is a value far away form your prediction (i.e. your forecast). To spot outliers, we will therefore analyze the forecast error and see which periods are *exceptionally wrong*. To do that, we'll use the standard deviation approach that we used previously.

Let's take back the example we made in table 10.5. We will compare the historical demand to a simple (but seasonal) forecast we have for it (see figure 10.7).

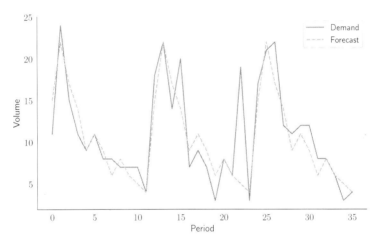

Figure 10.7: Seasonal demand

Month	M1	M2	M3	M4	M5	M6	M7	M8	M9	M10	M11	M12
Y1	11	24	15	11	9	11	8	8	7	7	7	4
Y2	18	22	14	20	7	9	7	3	8	6	19	3
Y3	17	21	22	12	11	12	12	8	8	6	3	4
Forecast	15	22	17	14	9	11	9	6	8	6	5	4

If we computed the error we have for such a forecast (which is simply an average of the historical demand), we would obtain a mean error of 0.4 and a standard deviation of 3.2 (this is of course heavily impacted by the error we have for Y2 M11). If we took a 99% confidence interval around this mean, we would shrink forecast errors into $-0.4 \pm 2.33 \times 3.2 = [-8, 7]$. You can see on figure 10.8 how these limits around the forecast perfectly fit the seasonal demand.

---

[1] Just like the Spanish Inquisition in Monty Python shows

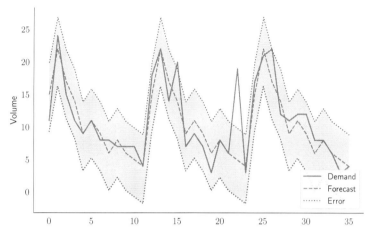

Figure 10.8: Outlier detection via forecast error

We can now correct our outlier from Y2 M11. The demand was 19 but the forecast was 5 for this period. The maximum *acceptable* value is then $5 + 7 = 12$. This means that we can replace the outlier of Y2 M11 (19) by this new value (12).

Conclusion With this smarter detection method – analyzing the forecast error deviation instead of simply the demand variation around the mean – we will be able to flag outliers much more precisely and reduce them back to a plausible amount. As you can see on figure 10.6, normalization and winsorization couldn't achieve any meaningful results for this seasonal demand.

The fine tuning of this method (*how many standard deviations should you take as a limit?*) is – of course – left to you to experiment...

Do It Yourself

Python If you have a pandas DataFrame with one column as the forecast and another one as the demand (the typical output from our exponential smoothing models), we can use this code:

```
df["Error"] = df["Forecast"] - df["Demand"]
m = df["Error"].mean()
s = df["Error"].std()

from scipy.stats import norm
```

```
 7  limit_high = norm.ppf(0.99,m,s)+df["Forecast"]
 8  limit_low = norm.ppf(0.01,m,s)+df["Forecast"]
 9  df["Updated"] = df["Demand"].clip(lower=limit_low,upper=limit_high)
10  print(df)
```

Go the extra mile!

If you think back about our idea to analyze the forecast error and make a threshold of acceptable errors, we actually still have a minor issue. The threshold we compute is based on the dataset including the outliers. This outlier drives the error variation upward so that the acceptable threshold is biased and overestimated. To correct this, one could actually shrink the outlier not to the threshold calculated based on the original demand dataset **but to a limit calculated on a dataset without this specific outlier**. Here's the recipe:

1. Populate a first forecast against the historical demand.
2. Compute the error, the error mean and the error standard deviation
3. Compute the lower & upper acceptable thresholds (based on the error mean and standard deviation).
4. Identify outliers just as explained previously.
5. Re-compute the error mean and standard deviation but excluding the outliers.
6. Update the lower & upper acceptable thresholds based on these new values.
7. Update the outlier values based on the new threshold.

If we take back our example from table 10.5, we initially had a forecast error mean of 0.4 and a standard deviation of 3.22. If we remove the point Y2 M11, we obtain an error mean of -0.1 and a standard deviation of 2.3. That means that now the thresholds are $[-5.3, 5.2]$ around the forecast. Our outlier in Y2 M11 would then be updated to 10 (instead of 12 with our previous technique).

Month	M1	M2	M3	M4	M5	M6	M7	M8	M9	M10	M11	M12
Y1	11	24	15	11	9	11	8	8	7	7	7	4
Y2	18	22	14	20	7	9	7	3	8	6	<u>19</u>	3
Y3	17	21	22	12	11	12	12	8	8	6	3	4
Forecast	15	22	17	14	9	11	9	6	8	6	5	4

Do It Yourself

We'll take back our code from our previous idea and add a new step to update the error mean and standard deviation values.

```
df["Error"] = df["Forecast"] - df["Demand"]
m = df["Error"].mean()
s = df["Error"].std()

from scipy.stats import norm
prob = norm.cdf(df["Error"], m, s)
outliers = (prob > 0.99) | (prob < 0.01)

m2 = df["Error"][~outliers].mean()
s2 = df["Error"][~outliers].std()

limit_high = norm.ppf(0.99,m2,s2)+df["Forecast"]
limit_low = norm.ppf(0.01,m2,s2)+df["Forecast"]
df["Updated"] = df["Demand"].clip(lower=limit_low,upper=limit_high)
print(df)
```

Chapter 11

Triple Additive Exponential smoothing

Idea

So far, we have discussed 4 different exponential smoothing models:

- Simple exponential smoothing ;
- Double exponential smoothing with (additive) trend;
- Double exponential smoothing with (additive) damped trend;
- Triple exponential smoothing with (additive) damped trend and multiplicative seasonality.

The last model we saw is very powerful but still has some limitations due to the multiplicative aspect of its seasonality. The issue of multiplicative seasonality is how the model reacts when you have periods with very low volumes. A period with a demand of 10 or 2 might have an absolute difference of 8 but there is actually a relative difference of 500%, so the seasonality (which is expressed in relative terms) could drastically change. We will then replace this multiplicative seasonality by an additive one.

With multiplicative seasonality, we could interpret the seasonal factors as a percentage increase (or decrease) of the demand during each period. One could say *"We sell 20% more in January but 30% less in February"*. Now, the seasonal factors will be absolute amounts to be added to the demand level. One could say *"We sell 150 units more than usual in January but 200 less in February"*.

Model

The global idea is that now the forecast is composed of the level plus the (damped) trend **plus** an additive seasonal factor s.

$$f_t = a_{t-1} + \phi b_{t-1} + s_{t-p}$$

Pay attention – like for the multiplicative model – we use the seasonal factors that were computed the previous season: s_{t-p} (where p denotes the season length – p for periodicity). We calculate the different components as such:

$$a_t = \alpha(d_t - s_{t-p}) \quad +(1-\alpha)(a_{t-1} + \phi b_{t-1})$$
$$b_t = \beta(a_t - a_{t-1}) \quad +(1-\beta)\phi b_{t-1}$$
$$s_t = \gamma(d_t - a_t) \quad +(1-\gamma)s_{t-p}$$

Note that the level and the trend are de-seasonalized. Whereas the forecast and the demand are seasonal. Again, s_{t-p} means that we use the seasonal factor as computed the last season.

Seasonal factors scaling

The seasonal factors must have an impact on how the forecast is spread across each period within a full seasonal cycle. But we do not want the seasonal factors to have an impact on the total forecast for the full cycle. For example, we want these seasonal factors to allocate more or less forecast to each month of a year, but the impact of the seasonal factors over the full year should be 0. If we sell 150 units more than usual in January, we should sell 150 units less than usual during the rest of the year.

If we translate this in mathematical terms, we have

$$\sum_{cycle} s = 0$$

This is important as it implies that the level, the forecast and the demand are on the same scale, as the sum of the seasonal factors over a full season cycle is 0^1.

---

[1] In practice – in order to simplify the seasonal factor update procedure – you can allow the seasonal factors to slightly drift away from p over time.

Seasonal factor initialization

Let's take back the initialization method we used for the multiplicative seasonality (i.e. initialize the seasonal weights based on the historical period – see page 73) and adapt it for additive seasonal factors.

1. **Computing the historical season averages.**
   Let's take back our dummy quarterly dataset:

	Y1	Y2	Y3	Y4	Y5	Mean
Q1	14	18	16	18	17	16.6
Q2	10	8	9	11	9	9.4
Q3	6	4	5	4	5	4.8
Q4	2	1	3	2	1	1.8

2. **Scaling the historical season averages.**
   We will scale our historical averages so that their sum will be equal to 0. In order to do this, we will **subtract** from our historical season averages their own mean (8.15).

	Y1	Y2	Y3	Y4	Y5	Mean	Factors
Q1	14	18	16	18	17	16.6	8.45
Q2	10	8	9	11	9	9.4	1.25
Q3	6	4	5	4	5	4.8	-3.35
Q4	2	1	3	2	1	1.8	-6.35
Mean						8.15	0.00

3. We now obtain a scaled set of seasonal factors: 8.45, 1.25, -3.35 & -6.35. They are now scaled as their sum and average is equal to 0. You can easily interpret them by saying that *"We sell 8.45 units more than usual in Q1 and 1.25 more than usual in Q2; in Q3 and Q4, we sell 3.35 and 6.35 units less than usual, respectively"*.

Just as for the multiplicative seasonal factors, if you have an important trend in the historical demand, you might face an issue and you should potentially first remove the trend in your data before computing the seasonal factors.

Other methods

Do not hesitate to apply the initialization methods we discussed for the multiplicative seasonal factors (page 75) to the additive seasonal factors. In any case, do not forget to scale the seasonal factors so that their sum is equal to 0.

Going further

If you are looking for more information on the different exponential smoothing models, you can check the online reference book "Forecasting: Principles and Practice" [11] which is freely available online on *otexts.org/fpp2*. It is written by Rob J Hyndman and George Athanasopoulos, two of the very best world-class leaders in the field of forecasting.

Insights

Comparison with the multiplicative model

Let's take back our example from the multiplicative triple model:

	Y1	Y2	Y3	Y4	Y5	Y6
Q1	14	18	16	18	17	?
Q2	10	8	9	11	9	?
Q3	6	4	5	4	5	?
Q4	2	1	3	2	1	?

Let's populate a forecast with our new additive model (with parameters *alpha* = 0.4, *beta* = 0.4, *phi* = 0.9 and *gamma* = 0.3) and see the differences compared to the multiplicative model.

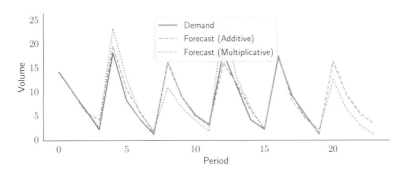

Figure 11.1: Additive forecast

As you can see on figure 11.1, the additive model is much more accurate than the multiplicative one (MAE of respectively 0.70 and 1.87) and gives a much more reasonable future prediction. Actually, if we look at how each model estimates the level of the demand (see figure 11.2), it is quite clear that the multiplicative model has an issue compared to the additive one.

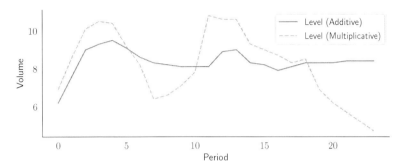

Figure 11.2: Level estimation

Limitations

Of course, as any other exponential smoothing model, a first limitation is the inability to deal with any external input (marketing budget, pricing impact...). But there is actually a second one. We will face an issue for the items with a significant trend.

Remember that the seasonality is defined by absolute amounts to be added to or removed from the (deseasonalized) level; so that if the level tends to grow (or shrink) over time, these absolute seasonal factors will not scale with the level. For example, let's imagine that on year 1 you have a product with an average demand of 10 pieces per month. You observe a seasonality ranging from -5 to +5. If you start to increase your sales at a rhythm of +10% per month as of Y2, soon your seasonality factors will be negligible compared to the demand level. The way the triple exponential smoothing model is defined does not allow for the seasonality to quickly evolve through time or to extrapolate changes! We actually want the seasonal factor to be rather stable over time.

This new additive model is actually **best suited for items with a stable demand or low demand**. The two seasonal models (additive and multiplicative) are complementary and should allow you to forecast any seasonal product. The best way to know which one you should use is of course to experiment.

Do It Yourself

Excel

We will take back our table that we made for the multiplicative model at the end of chapter 9 and change it for an additive model.

	A	B	C	D	E	F	G	H	I
1	Date	Demand	Forecast	Level (a)	Trend (b)	Season (s)		Alpha:	80%
2	1	14						Beta:	10%
3	2	10						Gamma:	40%
4	3	6							
5	4	2							
6	5	18							
7	6	8							
8	7	4							
9	8	1							

Level First we need to update the initialization, on the formula in cell D2, we will change (B3/F3) by (B3-F3). From there, we have to update the first year by updating the formula in cell D3 as below.

$$D3 = \$I\$1*(B3-F3)+(1-\$I\$1)*(D2+E2)$$

From here, you can copy it until D5. As of cell D6, you should then use:

$$D6 = \$I\$1*(B6-F2)+(1-\$I\$1)*(D5+E5)$$

Which we copy-paste until cell D21.

Trend We only need to initialize the trend in cell E2 as

$$E2 = (B3-F3)-(B2-F2)$$

No need to change the other formula as the trend is defined as for the multiplicative model.

Season Let's initialize our seasonal factors as $[8.5, 1.3, -3.4, -6.4]$ in cells F2:F5. In cell F6, you can use the formula

$$F6 = \$I\$3*(B6-D6)+(1-\$I\$3)*F2$$

which is the same as for the multiplicative model, except for the (B6-D6) part. You can then copy-paste this formula until the end of the historical period (cell F21).

Forecast It is now simply defined as the sum of the previous level trend and season. In cell C3, you can type D2+E2+F2 and copy-paste it until cell C5 (end of the first year). You can then define C6 as =D5+E5+F2 and copy-paste this until the end of the table.

Python

Seasonal factor initialization

Just like for the multiplicative model, let's first create a function to compute our additive seasonal factors. Do not hesitate to play with different initialization methods until you find the one that works best for you.

```python
def seasonal_factors_add(s,d,slen,cols):
    for i in range(slen):
        idx = [x for x in range(cols) if x%slen==i] # Compute indices that correspond to this season
        s[i] = np.mean(d[idx]) # Compute season average
    s -= np.mean(s[:slen]) # Scale season factors (sum of factors = 0)
    return s
```

Triple additive smoothing

Like for the other models, we will create a function called `triple_exp_smooth_add` that will take a time series `d` and a season length `slen` as input. The function takes as other optional inputs the different parameters `alpha`, `beta`, `gamma` & `phi` and the number of extra periods we want to forecast. The function will return a `pandas DataFrame` that will contain the historical demand, the forecast, the level, the trend, the seasonal factors and the forecast error.

```python
def triple_exp_smooth_add(d,slen=12,extra_periods=1, alpha=0.4, beta=0.4, phi=0.9,gamma=0.3):

    d = np.array(d) # Transform the input into a numpy array
    cols = len(d) # Historical period length
    d = np.append(d,[np.nan]*extra_periods) # Append np.nan into the demand array to cover future periods

    # components initialization
    f,a,b,s = np.full((4,cols+extra_periods),np.nan)
    s = seasonal_factors_add(s,d,slen,cols)

    # Level & Trend initialization
    a[0] = d[0]-s[0]
    b[0] = (d[1]-s[1]) - (d[0]-s[0])

    # Create the forecast for the first season
```

```
    for t in range(1,slen):
        f[t] = a[t−1] + phi*b[t−1] + s[t]
        a[t] = alpha*(d[t]−s[t]) + (1−alpha)*(a[t−1]+phi*b[t−1])
        b[t] = beta*(a[t]−a[t−1]) + (1−beta)*phi*b[t−1]

    # Create all the t+1 forecasts
    for t in range(slen,cols):
        f[t] = a[t−1] + phi*b[t−1] + s[t−slen]
        a[t] = alpha*(d[t]−s[t−slen]) + (1−alpha)*(a[t−1]+phi*b[t−1])
        b[t] = beta*(a[t]−a[t−1]) + (1−beta)*phi*b[t−1]
        s[t] = gamma*(d[t]−a[t]) + (1−gamma)*s[t−slen]

    # Forecast for all extra periods
    for t in range(cols,cols+extra_periods):
        f[t] = a[t−1] + phi*b[t−1] + s[t−slen]
        a[t] = f[t]−s[t−slen]
        b[t] = phi*b[t−1]
        s[t] = s[t−slen]

    df = pd.DataFrame.from_dict({"Demand":d,"Forecast":f,"Level":a,"Trend":b,"Season":s,"Error":d−f})

    return df
```

Once again, we can easily plot the model by simply calling `df.plot()` and we can easily calculate any forecast KPI by calling the appropriate function on `df.Error` (see the examples on page 83).

pandas – 2008

NumPy – 2005

Python – 1991

Damped trends – 1985
● ● ● ● ● ● ● ● ● ● ● ● ●

Winters – 1960
● ● ● ● ● ● ● ● ● ● ● ● ●
Holt – 1957
● ● ● ● ● ● ● ● ● ● ● ● ●

Python
Exponential Smoothing ● ● ● ● ● ● ● ● ● ● ● ● ●

Part II

Machine Learning

Chapter 12

Machine Learning

What is machine learning?

Until now, we have been using old-school statistics to predict demand; but with the recent rise of machine learning algorithms, we have new tools at our disposal that can easily achieve very good performance in terms of forecast accuracy for a typical industrial demand dataset. As you will see in the later chapters, these models will be able to learn many relationships that are beyond the ability of traditional exponential smoothing models. For example, we will discuss in chapters 20 & 22 how to add external information to our model.

So far, we have created different algorithms that used a predefined model to populate a forecast based on historical demand. The issue is that these models couldn't adapt to the historical demand. If you use a double exponential smoothing model to predict a seasonal product, it will fail to interpret the seasonal patterns. On the other hand, If you use a triple exponential smoothing model on a non-seasonal demand, it might overfit the noise of the demand and interpret it as a seasonality.

Machine learning is different: here, the algorithm (i.e. the machine) will learn relationships from a training dataset (i.e. our historical demand) and then be able to apply these relationships on new data. Whereas a traditional statistical model will apply a predefined relationship (model) to forecast the demand, a machine learning algorithm will not assume *a priori* a particular relationship (like a seasonality or a linear trend); it will **learn** these patterns directly from the historical demand.

For a machine learning algorithm to learn how to make predictions, we will have to show it both the inputs and the desired respective outputs. It will then automatically understand the relationships between these inputs and outputs.

Another important difference between using machine learning and exponential smoothing models to forecast our demand is the fact that a machine learning algorithm will **learn patterns from all our dataset**. Exponential smoothing models will treat each item individually, independently of the others. A machine learning algorithm will learn patterns from all the dataset and will apply what works best to each product. One could improve the accuracy of an exponential smoothing model by increasing the length of each time series (i.e. providing more historical periods for each product); but now, we will be able to increase the accuracy of our model by providing more products.

Welcome to the world of machine learning.

Machine learning for demand forecast

In order to make a forecast, the question we will ask the machine learning algorithm is the following:

Based on the last n periods of demand, what will the demand be during the next period(s)?

We will train the model by providing it the data with a specific layout:

- *n* consecutive periods of demand as input.
- the demand of the very next period(s) as output.

Let's see an example (with a quarterly forecast to simplify the table):

Product	Inputs				Output
	Q1	Q2	Q3	Q4	Q1 Y+1
#1	5	15	10	7	6
#2	7	2	3	1	4
#3	18	25	32	47	56
#4	4	1	5	3	3

Table 12.1: Data formatting for machine learning

For our forecast problem, we will basically show our machine learning algorithm different extracts of our historical demand dataset as inputs and each time show what the very next demand observation was. In our example above, the algorithm will learn the relationship between the last four quarters of demand and the demand of the next quarter. The algorithm will *learn* that if we have 5, 15, 10 & 7 as the last four demand observations, the next demand observation will be 6, so that its prediction should be 6.

Most people will react to this idea with two very different thoughts. Either people will think that *"it is simply impossible for a computer to look at the demand and make a prediction"* or that *"as of now, the humans have nothing left to do"*. Both are wrong.

As we will see later, machine learning can generate very accurate predictions. And as the human controlling the machine, we still have to ask ourselves many questions:

- Which data to feed the algorithm for it to understand the proper relationships.
- Which machine learning algorithm to use (there are many different ones!).
- Which parameters to use in our model. As you will see, each machine learning algorithm has some parameters that we can tweak to improve its accuracy.

As always, there is no definitive one-size-fits-all answer. Experimentation will help you find what is best for your dataset.

Data preparation

The first step of any machine learning algorithm project is to properly clean and format the data. In our case, we need to format the historical demand dataset to obtain one similar to table 12.1.

Naming convention During our data cleaning process, we will use the standard data science notation and call the inputs X and the outputs Y. Specifically, the datasets X_train & Y_train will contain all the historical demand we will use to **train** our algorithm (X_train being the inputs and Y_train the outputs). And the datasets X_test & Y_test will be used to **test** our model.

You can see on table 12.2 an example of a typical historical demand dataset you should have at the beginning of a forecast project.

Product	Y1				Y2				Y3			
	Q1	Q2	Q3	Q4	Q1	Q2	Q3	Q4	Q1	Q2	Q3	Q4
#1	5	15	10	7	6	13	11	5	4	11	9	4
#2	7	2	3	1	1	0	0	1	3	2	4	5
#3	18	25	32	47	56	70	64	68	72	67	65	58
#4	4	1	5	3	2	5	3	1	4	3	2	5

Table 12.2: Typical example of historical demand dataset

We now have to format this dataset to something similar to table 12.1. Let's say for now that we want to predict the demand of a product during one quarter based on the demand observations of this product during the previous four quarters[1]. We will populate the datasets X_train & Y_train by going through the different products we have and each time create a data sample with four consecutive quarters as X_train and the following quarter as Y_train. This way, the machine learning algorithm will learn the relationship(s) between one quarter of demand and the previous four.

You can see on table 12.3 an illustration for the first iterations. In order to validate our model, we will keep Y3Q4 aside as a test set.

Loop	Product	Y1				Y2				Y3			
		Q1	Q2	Q3	Q4	Q1	Q2	Q3	Q4	Q1	Q2	Q3	Q4
#1	#1	5	15	10	7	6							
#1	#2	7	2	3	1	1							
#1	#3	18	25	32	47	56							
#1	#4	4	1	5	3	2							
#2	#1		15	10	7	6	13						
#2	#2		2	3	1	1	0						
#2	#3		25	32	47	56	70						
#2	#4		1	5	3	2	5						
#3	#1			10	7	6	13	11					
...	...			...	...	...	...	...					

Table 12.3: Training and test-set creation

Note that our training set won't go until Y3Q4 as **it is kept for the test set**: the last loop will be used as a final test.

Our X_train and Y_train datasets will look like table 12.4.

Remember that our algorithm will learn relationships in X_train to predict Y_train. So we could write that as X_train → Y_train.

---

[1] We'll discuss variations of this in chapter 18.

Data preparation

Loop	Product	X_train				→	Y_train
#1	#1	5	15	10	7	→	6
#1	#2	7	2	3	1	→	1
#1	#3	18	25	32	47	→	56
#1	#4	4	1	5	3	→	2
#2	#1	15	10	7	6	→	13
#2	#2	2	3	1	1	→	0
#2	#3	25	32	47	56	→	70
...	...	...	...	...	...	→	...

Table 12.4: X_train & Y_train

The final test will be given to our tool via these X_test & Y_test datasets:

X_test				Y_test
5	4	11	9	4
1	3	2	4	5
68	72	67	65	58
1	4	3	2	5

These are each time the four latest demand quarters we know for each item just before Y3Q4 (i.e. Y2Q4 to Y3Q3). That means that our algorithm won't see these relationships during its training phase as it will be tested on the accuracy it achieved on these specific prediction exercises. We will measure its accuracy on this test set and assume its accuracy when predicting future demand will be similar.

Dataset length

It is important for any machine learning exercise to pay attention to how much data is fed to the algorithm. The more, the better. On the other hand, the more periods we use to do a prediction (we will call this x_len), the less we will be able to loop through the dataset. Also, if we want to predict more periods at once (y_len), it will also cost us a part of the dataset, as we need more data (Y_train is longer) to perform one loop in our dataset.

Typically, if we have a dataset with n periods, we will be able to make $1 + n - $ x_len $ - $ y_len runs through it.

$$loops = 1 + n - x\_len - y\_len$$

It is a best practice to keep at the very least enough runs to loop through two full years so that $23 + x\_len + y\_len \leq n$. This means that the algorithm will have two full seasonal cycles to learn any possible relationships. If it had just one, you would be facing high risks of overfitting.

Do It Yourself

Data collection

The dataset creation and cleaning is a very important part of any data science project. In order to illustrate all the models we will create in the next chapters, we will use the historical sales of cars in Norway from January 2007 to January 2017 as an example dataset. You can download this dataset here:

$$www.supchains.com/download$$

You will get a csv file called norway_new_car_sales_by_make.csv. This dataset contains the sales of 65 car makers accross 121 months. On average, a bit more than 140 000 new cars are sold in Norway per year, so that the market can then be roughly estimated to be worth 4B$ if we assume that the price of a new car is on average around 30 000$ in Norway. This dataset is modest in terms of size, but it is big enough to be relevant to experiment with new models and ideas. Nevertheless, machine learning models might show better results on other bigger datasets.

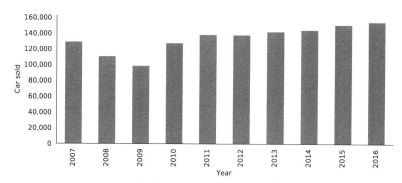

Figure 12.1: Cars sold per year in Norway

Bring Your Own Data Set In the next chapters, we will discuss various different models and apply them to this example dataset. But what we are actually interested in is **your own dataset**. Do not waste any time and already start to gather some historical demand data so that you can test the following models on your own historical demand data as we progress through the different topics. It is recommended that you start with a dataset with at least 3 years of data (5 would be better) and more than a hundred different products. The bigger, the better.

Training and test sets creation

We will make a first code to extract the data from this csv and format it with the dates as columns and the products as lines.

```python
# Load the CSV file (should be in the same directory)
data = pd.read_csv("norway_new_car_sales_by_make.csv")

# Create a column "Period" with both the Year and the Month
data["Period"] = data["Year"].astype(str) + "-" + data["Month"].astype(str)
# We use the datetime formatting to make sure format is consistent
data["Period"] = pd.to_datetime(data["Period"]).dt.strftime("%Y-%m")

# Create a pivot of the data to show the periods on columns and the car makers on rows
df = pd.pivot_table(data=data, values="Quantity", index="Make", columns="Period", aggfunc='sum', fill_value=0)

# Print data to Excel for reference
df.to_excel("Clean Demand.xlsx")
```

Note that we print the results in an Excel file for later reference. It is always good practice to visually check what the dataset looks like to be sure the code worked as intended.

You can also define a function to store these steps for later use.

```python
def import_data():
    data = pd.read_csv("norway_new_car_sales_by_make.csv")
    data["Period"] = data["Year"].astype(str) + "-" + data["Month"].astype(str)
    data["Period"] = pd.to_datetime(data["Period"]).dt.strftime("%Y-%m")
    df = pd.pivot_table(data=data,values="Quantity",index="Make", columns="Period",aggfunc='sum',fill_value=0)
    return df
```

Now that we have our dataset with the proper formatting, we can create our training and test sets. For this purpose, we will create a function datasets that takes as inputs:

    df our initial historical demand;

    x_len the number of months we will use to make a prediction;

    y_len the number of months we want to predict;

y_test_len the number of months we leave as a final test;

and returns X_train, Y_train, X_test & Y_test.

```python
def datasets(df, x_len=12, y_len=1, y_test_len=12):

    D = df.values
    periods = D.shape[1]

    # Training set creation: run through all the possible time windows
    loops = periods + 1 - x_len - y_len - y_test_len
    train = []
    for col in range(loops):
        train.append(D[:,col:col+x_len+y_len])
    train = np.vstack(train)
    X_train, Y_train = np.split(train,[x_len],axis=1)

    # Test set creation: unseen "future" data with the demand just before
    max_col_test = periods - x_len - y_len + 1
    test = []
    for col in range(loops,max_col_test):
        test.append(D[:,col:col+x_len+y_len])
    test = np.vstack(test)
    X_test, Y_test = np.split(test,[x_len],axis=1)

    # this data formatting is needed if we only predict a single period
    if y_len == 1:
        Y_train = Y_train.ravel()
        Y_test = Y_test.ravel()

    return X_train, Y_train, X_test, Y_test
```

In our function, we have to use .ravel() on both Y_train and Y_test if we only want to predict one period at a time.

array.ravel() reduces the dimension of a NumPy array to 1D.

Y_train and Y_test are always created by our function as 2D arrays (i.e. arrays with rows and columns). If we only want to predict one period at a time, these arrays will then only have one column (and multiple rows). Unfortunately, the functions we will use later will want 1D arrays if we want to forecast only one period.

We can now easily call our new function datasets(df) as well as import_data().

```python
import numpy as np
import pandas as pd
```

Do It Yourself

```
3
4  df = import_data()
5  X_train, Y_train, X_test, Y_test = datasets(df)
```

We now obtain the datasets we need to feed our machine learning algorithm (X_train & Y_train) and the datasets we need to test it (X_test & Y_test).

Note that we took y_test_len as 12 periods. That means we will test our algorithm over 12 different predictions (as we only predict one period at a time).

Forecasting multiple periods at once You can change y_len if you want to forecast multiple periods at once. You need to pay attention to keep y_test_len $\geq$ y_len, otherwise you won't be able to test all the predictions of your algorithm. In the following chapters, we will keep y_len = 1 for the sake of simplicity.

What about Excel? So far, Excel could provide us an easy way to see the data and our statistical model relationships. But it won't get us any further. Unfortunately, Excel does not provide the power to *easily* format such datasets into the different parts we need (X_train, X_test, Y_train & Y_test). Moreover, with most of our machine learning models, the dataset size will get too big for Excel to handle correctly. Actually, another major blocking point is that Excel does not provide any machine learning algorithm.

Benchmark

Now that we have created our training and test sets, let's create a forecast benchmark. We want to have an indication of what a simple model could do in order to compare its accuracy against our more complex models. Basically, if a model got an error of *x* percent, we will compare this against the error of our benchmark in order to know if *x* is a good result or not.

We will use a simple linear regression as a benchmark. If you are not familiar with the concept of linear regression, you can just picture it as a straight line that will match historical demand and project it into the future. Many Python libraries propose models to compute linear regressions, but we will choose `scikit-learn` as we will later use this library for all our machine learning models. Let's stay consistent from one model to another.

```python
from sklearn.linear_model import LinearRegression

reg = LinearRegression() # Create a linear regression object
reg = reg.fit(X_train,Y_train) # Fit it to the training data

# Create two predictions for the training and test sets
Y_train_pred = reg.predict(X_train)
Y_test_pred = reg.predict(X_test)
```

As you can see, we created a model object `reg` that we fitted to our training data (`X_train,Y_train`) thanks to the method `.fit()`. We then populated a prediction based on `X_train` and `X_test` via the method `.predict(X_train)` (respectively `.predict(X_test)`).

We can now compare these forecasts against the actual values.

```python
# Compute MAE for both the training and test sets
MAE_train = np.mean(abs(Y_train - Y_train_pred))/np.mean(Y_train)
MAE_test = np.mean(abs(Y_test - Y_test_pred))/np.mean(Y_test)

# Print the results
print("Regression Train MAE%:",round(MAE_train*100,1))
print("Regression Test MAE%:",round(MAE_test*100,1))
```

And this is what we obtain

```
Regression Train MAE%: 17.8
Regression Test MAE%: 17.8
```

Car sales are actually easy to forecast and rather stable products without seasonality. This is why the linear benchmark provides such good results here. On top of that, we only predict one month at a time and linear approximation works well in the short term. On a different dataset, with a longer forecast horizon (and maybe some seasonality), linear regressions might not be up to the challenge.

Now that we have a proper dataset and a benchmark to beat, let's see how far machine learning can get us.

Chapter 13

Tree

As a first machine learning algorithm, we will use a **decision tree**. Decision trees are a class of machine learning algorithms that will create a map (a tree actually) of questions to make a prediction. We call these trees **regression trees** if we want them to predict a number, or **classification trees** if we want them to predict a category or a label.

In order to make a prediction, the tree will start at its foundation with a first yes/no question, and based on the answer it will continue asking new yes/no questions until it gets to a final prediction. Somehow you could see these trees as a big game of "Guess Who?" (the famous '80s game): the model will ask multiple consecutive questions until it gets to a good answer.

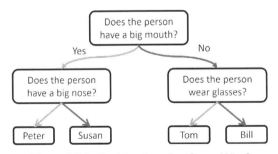

Figure 13.1: Decision tree for *Guess Who?*

In a decision tree, each question is called a **node**. For example, on figure 13.1 *"Does the person have a big nose?"* is a node. Each possible final answer is called a **leaf**. On figure 13.1 each leaf contains only one single person. But that is not mandatory. You could imagine that multiple people have a big mouth and a big nose. In such case, the leaf would contain multiple values.

The different pieces of information that a tree has at its disposal to split a node are called the **features**. For example, the tree we had on figure 13.1 for the game *Guess who?* could split a node on the three features "Mouth", "Nose" and "Glasses".

How does it work?

To illustrate how our tree will grow, let's take back our quarterly dummy dataset.

	X_train				Y_train
5	15	10	7		6
15	10	7	6		13
10	7	6	13		11
7	6	13	11		5
6	13	11	5		4
13	11	5	4		11
11	5	4	11		9
7	2	3	1		1

Based on this training dataset, a **smart** question to ask yourself in order to make a prediction is: *Is the first demand observation >7?*

	X_train			Y_train	Is the first demand observation >7?
5	15	10	7	6	No
15	10	7	6	**13**	Yes
10	7	6	13	**11**	Yes
7	6	13	11	5	No
6	13	11	5	4	No
13	11	5	4	**11**	Yes
11	5	4	11	**9**	Yes
7	2	3	1	1	No

This is a smart question as you know that the answer (Yes/No) will provide an interesting indication on the behaviour of the demand for the next quarter. If the answer is *yes*, the demand we try to predict is likely to be rather high (≥ 8) and if the answer is *no*, then the demand we try to predict is likely to be low (≤ 7).

Here is an example with a **bad** question.

How does it work?

X_train				Y_train	Is the third demand observation <6?
5	15	10	7	6	No
15	10	7	6	13	No
10	7	6	13	11	No
7	6	13	11	5	No
6	13	11	5	4	No
13	11	5	4	11	Yes
11	5	4	11	9	Yes
7	2	3	1	1	Yes

This does not really help as this question does not separate our dataset into two different subsets (i.e. there is still a lot of variation inside each subset). If the answer to the question *Is the third demand observation <6?* is *yes*, we still have a range of demand going from 1 to 11 and if the answer is *no* the range goes from 4 to 13. This question is simply not helpful to forecast future demand.

Without going too much into details of the tree's mathematical inner workings, the algorithm to grow our tree will, at each node, choose a question (i.e. a **split**) about one of the available **features** (i.e. the previous quarters) that will minimize the prediction error across the two new data subsets. The first algorithm proposed to create a decision tree was published in 1963 by Morgan and Sonquist in their paper "Problems in the Analysis of Survey Data and a Proposal" [9]. There are many different algorithms on how to grow a decision tree (many were developed since the '60s), but they all follow the objective of asking the most meaningful questions about the different features of a dataset in order to split it into different subsets until some criterion is reached.

Parameters

It's important to realize that without a criterion to stop the growth of our tree, it will grow until each data observation (otherwise called **sample**) has its own leaf. This is a really bad idea as even though you will have a perfect accuracy on your training set, you will not be able to replicate these results on new data. We will limit the growth of our tree based on some criterion. Let's take a look at the most important ones (we are already using the `scikit-learn` naming convention).

>**Max depth** Maximum amount of consecutive questions (nodes) the tree can ask.

Min samples split Minimum amount of samples that are required in a node to trigger a new split. If you set this to 6, a node with only 5 observations left won't be split further.

Min samples leaf Minimum amount of observations that need to be in a leaf. This is a very important parameter. The closer this is to 0, the higher the risk of overfitting, as your tree will actually grow until it asks enough questions to treat each observation separately.

Of course, depending on your dataset, you might want to give different values to these parameters. We will discuss how to choose the best parameters in the following chapter.

Do It Yourself

We will use the scikit-learn Python library (www.scikit-learn.org) to grow our first tree. This is a well-known open-source library that is used all over the world by data scientists. It is built on top of NumPy, so that it interacts easily with the rest of our code.

The first step is to call the scikit-learn library and create an instance of a regression tree. Once this is done, we have to train it based on our X_train and Y_train arrays.

```
from sklearn.tree import DecisionTreeRegressor

# -- Instantiate a Decision Tree Regressor
tree = DecisionTreeRegressor(max_depth=5,min_samples_leaf=5)

# -- Fit the tree to the training data
tree.fit(X_train,Y_train)
```

Note that we created a tree with a maximum depth of 5 (i.e. maximum 5 yes/no consecutive questions are asked to classify one point), where each tree leaf has at minimum 5 samples.

We now have a tree trained to our specific demand history. We can already measure its accuracy on the training dataset.

```
# Create a prediction based on our model
Y_train_pred = tree.predict(X_train)

# Compute the Mean Absolute Error of the model
import numpy as np
MAE_tree = np.mean(abs(Y_train − Y_train_pred))/np.mean(Y_test)
```

Do It Yourself

```
7
8  # Print the results
9  print("Tree on train set MAE%:",round(MAE_tree*100,1))
```

You should obtain an MAE of 15.1%. Now let's measure the accuracy against the test set:

```
1  Y_test_pred = tree.predict(X_test)
2  MAE_test = np.mean(abs(Y_test - Y_test_pred))/np.mean(Y_test)
3  print("Tree on test set MAE%:",round(MAE_test*100,1))
```

We now obtain around 21.1%. This means that our regression tree is overfitted to the historical demand: we lost 6 points of MAE in the test set compared to the historical dataset.

Our benchmark (the linear regression we did at the end of chapter 12) obtained an error of 17.8%! Which means that our regression tree is (unfortunately) less good than a simple linear regression.

Before we look at how we can improve this further, let's discuss MAE and RMSE.

MAE vs RMSE

We discussed in chapter 2 the advantages (and disadvantages) of using either the root mean square error (RMSE) or the mean absolute error (MAE) as a KPI to asses our forecast accuracy. Thanks to `scikit-learn` we can choose to optimize our tree to minimize one or the other[1] (thanks to the parameter `criterion`). Unfortunately, due to the inner workings of the algorithm used to grow regression trees, the optimization for MAE is going to take much longer than the one for RMSE.

Let's record how long it takes to optimize a tree that minimizes MAE and another one that minimizes MSE. In order to do so, we will use the `time` library which can give us the current time via `time.time()`.

```
1  import time
2  for criterion in ["mse","mae"]:
3      start_time = time.time()
4      tree = DecisionTreeRegressor(max_depth=5,min_samples_leaf=5,
            criterion=criterion)
```

---

[1] Actually most of the machine learning algorithms optimize the mean square error (MSE) rather than the root mean square error as it is easier to compute and manipulate.

```
 5      tree.fit(X_train,Y_train)
 6      Y_test_pred = tree.predict(X_test)
 7      MAE_test = np.mean(abs(Y_test - Y_test_pred))/np.mean(Y_test)
 8      print(criterion)
 9      print("%s seconds" % round(time.time() - start_time,2))
10      print("MAE%:",round(MAE_test*100,2))
11      print()
```

These are the results we obtain:

```
1  mse
2  0.01 seconds
3  MAE%: 21.08
4
5  mae
6  0.86 seconds
7  MAE%: 21.64
```

As you can see, on this dataset, MAE optimization is around 100x slower than MSE optimization. This difference might even grow bigger as our dataset grows. This means that unfortunately, to optimize our tree (and later our forest and extremely randomized trees), we will need to stick to MSE instead of MAE. Note that, by default, `scikit-learn` uses MSE to fit its different models.

Another interesting aspect is that the optimization for MAE results in a slightly worse MAE on the final test set than the one for MSE. This is surprising but not unusual, as we haven't optimized our parameters yet and we can have from time to time a dataset that is much more fitted to MSE or to MAE. Once again, only experimentation will tell.

Chapter 14

Parameter Optimization

When we created our regression tree in chapter 13, we chose some parameters:

```
tree = DecisionTreeRegressor(max_depth=5, min_samples_leaf=5)
```

But are we sure these are the best? Maybe if we set max_depth to 7 we could improve our model accuracy? It is unfortunately impossible to know *a priori* what the best set of parameters is. But that's fine, we are supply chain data scientists, we love to run experiments.

We will create a code to run through different values for the maximum depth, test each of them and select the best one.

Simple experiment

As you can see on figure 14.1, increasing the maximum depth of our tree (i.e. allowing it to ask more consecutive questions) continuously improves the accuracy over the training set. But we reach a plateau for the test set accuracy at around 6. Actually, the accuracy on the test set is even a bit worse if the maximum depth is 14 rather than 6. It is important here to understand that if we choose a model with a maximum depth around 8 or more, we will have a model that is **highly overfitted** to the training set and won't perform well on the test set. So should we choose max_depth=6 and call it a day? No.

If we did this, we would actually be optimizing this parameter directly against the test set. We would then face the risk of overfitting the model

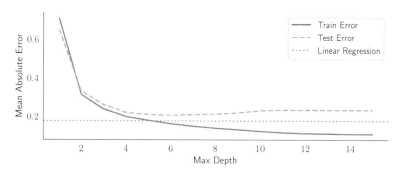

Figure 14.1: Experimentation for maximum depth

to the test set and not being able to replicate similar results against new data.

Risk of overfitting

Our initial idea to optimize a parameter was to train all the potential parameter sets on the training set and keep the one that performed best against our test set.

This was a very bad idea. You would get very good **but artifical** results. Remember that the test set should only be used to validate the results of your model at the very end of the process, not to select a set of parameters. If you do that, you are actually optimizing your model to fit the test set.

We will then have to use another experiment that does not require us to use our test set.

Smarter experiments

Let's design a new experimentation method that is both efficient and doesn't risk overfitting. This method will rely on two concepts:

cross-validation To avoid overfitting.

Random Search To efficiently find a (very) good parameter set among different possibilities.

Smarter experiments

K-fold cross-validation

K-fold cross-validation is a validation technique to assess a model's accuracy over a dataset without overfitting. Here's how it works:

1. Divide our (training!) dataset into k different subsets (each of them is called a **fold**).
2. Train our model based on all the folds but one.
3. Use the remaining fold as a **validation** dataset to assess the model's performance.
4. As we have k folds, we can repeat steps two and three k times (each time changing the validation set) and keep the average performance obtained as the final result.

Here is an example with $k = 5$. We have an initial dataset from which we cut two parts: the training set (and 5 subsets) and the test set.

Training Set					Test Set
Fold #1	Fold #2	Fold #3	Fold #4	Fold #5	Final test set

Based on our initial training set, we can then run 5 different experiments. For each of them, we will train the model with 4 folds and keep the fifth one to test its performance. We'll call this 5th fold the **validation dataset**.

Experiment	Training Set				Validation Set
#1	Fold #1	Fold #2	Fold #3	Fold #4	Fold #5
#2	Fold #2	Fold #3	Fold #4	Fold #5	Fold #1
#3	Fold #3	Fold #4	Fold #5	Fold #1	Fold #2
#4	Fold #4	Fold #5	Fold #1	Fold #2	Fold #3
#5	Fold #5	Fold #1	Fold #2	Fold #3	Fold #4

We will then measure the accuracy of our model as the average accuracy achieved against the validation set over each of these experiments. The best model is then kept and its accuracy finally measured against the original (final) test set.

Our new k-fold cross-validation method allows us to test many different parameter sets and keep the best one without overfitting. Remember that with the cross-validation method we keep the best model based on results achieved over different validation sets which are all part of the initial training dataset. That means that **we optimize our model directly on the training set and leave the test set for the final results**.

Grid Search

Now that we have a method to test different parameter sets against a training set, we should ask ourselves the question: *which parameter sets should we try?* As the complexity of our model grows, we will have more and more different parameters that need to be optimized. We cannot optimize each parameter independently of the others as there might be an interaction between them, so that we could actually come up with thousands (millions?) of possible different parameter sets. We then have to find a smart way to test *some* parameter sets and keep the best one.

Uniform search

The first straightforward idea is to define a space with all the possible values for each parameter we want to try. We can then test a certain number of possibilities of this space by uniformly choosing points among it (see figure 14.2).

Let's imagine a very simple example where you want to choose the best parameters among two inputs (Max_depth and Min_samples_split). You assume that Max_depth could vary between 5 and 15, and that Min_samples_split could vary between 2 and 12. As you have 11 potential values for each parameter, that's a total of 121 different models to test. If you only have the time to test 25 models out of these 121 possibilities, you would uniformly spread these tests among the space of possibilities as shown on figure 14.2.

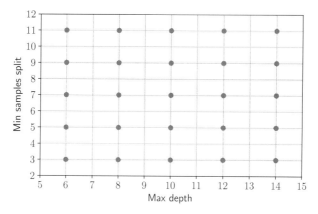

Figure 14.2: Grid Search

Smarter experiments

This uniform search is a fair technique to look for a good parameter set among many possibilities. But actually, there is a smarter – yet less obvious – way.

Random search

The second idea is to cover the space of possibilities **not by searching uniformly** among the parameters but **by random spot tests**. One could think that this is a bad idea as we risk missing an interesting output by lack of chance. But there is actually a very interesting fact about this technique. With the uniform search example above, you would only test 5 different values for each parameter, but if you take each test at random, you might test many more values for each parameter. On figure 14.3, you can see that by doing 25 random tests, we tried 10 different values for Max_depth and 9 different values for Min_samples_split.

Now imagine that the influence of one parameter is less important than the other (but we do not know *a priori* which one); in such a situation, with the random search you will have tested around more different values of the interesting parameter than with the uniform technique. Of course, this example with only two parameters is rather simple. As you will have to optimize more and more parameters at once, this effect will become more and more important, as some parameters will be much more important than others.

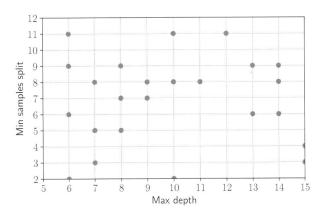

Figure 14.3: Random Search

Last piece of advice I recommend you search for the best set of parameters in a two-step approach:

1. Start by doing a random search on a broad space of parameters;
2. Launch a new search on a more refined space around the best value found on step 1.

This should help you to cover a lot of space efficiently and still not to miss a very good value.

Do It Yourself

Actually, this kind of experimentation is really easy to make with `scikit-learn` as the library has very useful functions to perform random search and k-fold cross-validation automatically.

We will start by creating arrays that will contain all the parameter sets we want to test.

```
max_depth = list(range(5,11))
max_depth.append(None)
min_samples_leaf = range(5,20)
param_dist = {"max_depth": max_depth,
              "min_samples_leaf": min_samples_leaf}
```

Note that we store these parameters inside a `dictionary` that will be later used when we call `RandomizedSearchCV()`. You can of course change the parameter range.

We also append `None` to `max_depth`. If the maximum depth of a tree is set to `None`, it simply means that the tree is not restricted by any maximum depth. In our case, the only restriction left will be the minimum samples per leaf.

We can then launch our experiment and test all these different parameter sets against our training set.

```
from sklearn.tree import DecisionTreeRegressor
from sklearn.model_selection import RandomizedSearchCV
tree = DecisionTreeRegressor()
tree_cv = RandomizedSearchCV(tree, param_dist, n_jobs=-1, cv=10,
     verbose=1, n_iter=100, scoring="neg_mean_absolute_error")
tree_cv.fit(X_train,Y_train)
print("Tuned Regression Tree Parameters:",tree_cv.best_params_)
```

Do It Yourself

We start by creating a tree instance. Then we create an instance of a `RandomizedSearchCV` object. This object takes as an input a specific model type (here our tree) and a parameter distribution (that we did above). We can also feed it other parameters:

n_jobs (int, default=1)
This very useful parameter is the number of processors Python will allocate to run the model. Each processor will work in parallel to run a different tree. You can set it to n_jobs=-1 to allocate all your processors (and drastically reduce the computation time!).

cv (int, default = 3)
This is the number of folds we want to create (the k factor from the k-fold cross-validation).

verbose (int, default = 0)
The higher the parameter, the more information the function will provide on the console when you launch it.

n_iter (int, default = 10)
This is the number of parameter sets you want to test. The higher, the better, as you will test more different parameter sets. But this will be done at the expense of a longer computation time.

scoring (string, default None)
This gives the scoring metric (i.e. KPI) that will be used to select the best model. Typically, we want to use either neg_mean_absolute_error which is MAE or neg_mean_squared_error for MSE. Note that there is a difference between this `scoring` that is used to select the best model among all the ones that were tested and the `criterion` that is used as a KPI to optimize each tree individually. Basically, this means that we can optimize our trees for MSE (via `criterion`) and then select the one that got the best MAE (via `scoring`).

The function will then print the best parameters that it has found. Finally, you can display the accuracy achieved over the training and the test sets:

```
Y_train_pred = tree_cv.predict(X_train)
MAE_test = np.mean(abs(Y_train − Y_train_pred))/np.mean(Y_train)
print("Tree on training set MAE%:",round(MAE_test*100,1))

Y_test_pred = tree_cv.predict(X_test)
MAE_test = np.mean(abs(Y_test − Y_test_pred))/np.mean(Y_test)
print("Tree on test set MAE%:",round(MAE_test*100,1))
```

On our example, we got these results:

```
Fitting 10 folds for each of 100 candidates, totalling 1000 fits
Tuned Regression Tree Parameters: {'min_samples_leaf': 18, 'max_depth': 7}
Tree on training set MAE%: 16.8
Tree on test set MAE%: 18.1
[Parallel(n_jobs=-1)]: Done 1000 out of 1000 | elapsed: 3.9s finished
```

See on table 14.1 how the accuracy on the test set improved from 21.1% on our original tree to 18.1%. This is much better of course, but still less than a simple linear regression.

	Training	Test
Regression	17.8	17.8
Tree (not optimized)	15.1	21.1
Tree (optimized)	16.8	18.1

Table 14.1: Results

Note that the accuracy on the training set is now around 17%. So still much lower than our test set results. In order to reduce the overfitting a bit, we could do the randomized search on a larger space of parameters along with a high number of k-fold (cv=10 is already considered as a high value) but this will drastically increase the computation time. Unfortunately, we will never be able to totally take this overfitting away. As discussed in chapter 8, we will face this issue more and more as we use more complex models.

Recap

As machine learning models have many parameters, we learned how to combine a random search with a k-fold cross-validation, which is a powerful and easy way to test many different parameter sets with a limited risk of overfitting. As we could test many parameter sets, we improved the performance of our tree. But not enough to beat the benchmark yet.

Let's see what else we can do.

Chapter 15

Forest

In the social choice theory[1], there is a concept called **the wisdom of the crowd**. This idea explains that the average opinion of a group of people is going to be more precise on average that the opinion of a single member of the group. Let's give a simple example, if you want to make a forecast for the demand of a product next month, it is better to ask the opinion of many different team members (sales people, marketing, CEO, supply chain planners, financial analysts) and take the average of the different forecasts rather than to blindly trust only one team member.

In their (Excellent) book "Superforecasting: The Art and Science of Prediction" [10] Philip E. Tetlock and Dan Gardner explain how one can harness the power of the wisdom of the crowd among a team to predict anything from stock-price value to presidential elections.

Can we use this concept with our tree? Yes, of course.

Random trees in a forest

In 1995, in his article "Random Decision Forests" [6] Tin Kan Ho proposed a new idea to bring the power of the wisdom of the crowd to regression trees. Let's imagine that we could from our initial training dataset populate different regression trees. All accurate but all slightly different. Being different is what makes them all relevant. We could then make a better

---

[1] The social choice theory is the science of combining different individual choices into a final global decision. These questions initiated with the voting paradox in the late 18th century stating that a collective preference of a group can be cyclic even if none of the preferences of each individual are cyclic.

prediction by taking the average of the predictions of all the different trees. We will call this ensemble of regression trees a...
Forest!

Let's discuss how we can create (slightly) different (accurate) regression trees from a single training dataset.

Idea #1 – Bootstrapping Bootstrapping means that we will create a unique random training dataset for each single tree. Each tree will receive a random selection of the initial training dataset based on a selection with replacement. That means that in the dataset of each tree, you could find some similar data points multiple times and you could miss some other data points. Each tree will receive a dataset that will be as big as the initial training set.

Idea #2 – Restrain the maximum amount of features Do you remember that the regression tree will choose at each node the best feature (i.e. input) to create a split on? If we limit the maximum number of features (`max_features` in `scikit-learn`) the algorithm can choose from at each node, and the features are each time chosen randomly, **we will then obtain different trees at each fitting**. What is interesting by restricting how the different trees can grow, is that they become more different from each other (even if it is done at the expense of their own accuracy) than simply with bootstrapping.

Do It Yourself

Random Forest

We will import the `RandomForestRegressor` from the `sklearn.ensemble` library. The `ensemble` library means that these models are actually based on an ensemble of sub-models.

```
from sklearn.ensemble import RandomForestRegressor

forest = RandomForestRegressor(bootstrap=True, max_features="auto",
    min_samples_leaf=18, max_depth=7)
forest.fit(X_train,Y_train)
```

See how easy it is to create one forest thanks to `sklearn`.

Do It Yourself

Let's take a look at the accuracy before we discuss the different parameters:

```
Y_test_pred = forest.predict(X_test)
MAE_test = np.mean(abs(Y_test - Y_test_pred))/np.mean(Y_test)
print("Forest on test set MAE%:",round(MAE_test*100,1))
```

This is what we obtain:

```
Forest on test set MAE%: 17.9
```

We now obtain an accuracy of around 17.9% of MAE. This is better than our previous tree that was around 18.1%, but still less good than our benchmark of 17.8%.
Now that we have a working model, let's discuss the different parameters.

Parameters

Before we improve our model further, let's take some time to discuss the different parameters.

bootstrap (boolean, default = True)
This parameter indicates if the random forest will use bootstrapping. As explained above, bootstrapping allows each tree to grow differently as they use slightly different training datasets. It is then advised to keep this to True.

max_depth (int, default = none)
Just as for the regular tree, this is the maximum depth (i.e. maximum number of consecutive yes/no questions) of each tree.

max_features (int or float, default = n_features)
This is the maximum amount of features a tree can choose from when it has to split a node. Note that the set of available features to choose from randomly changes at each node. As explained above, it is important to create some variations among the different trees and the feature restriction is a good way to create this randomness.
Pay attention that if **max_features** is input as an integer (e.g. 1, 2, 10...), this will be the exact number of features to be selected. If it is input as a float from 0.0 to 1.0^{1}, this ratio will be applied to the total number of features in the dataset. For example, **max_features=0.5** means that you want the maximum number of features to be equal

---
[1]Pay attention that 1 will be considered as an integer and 1.0 as a float. You can expect totally different results.

to half of the dataset features; `max_features=1.0` means that you want the maximum number of features to be equal to the number of features (that is to say that there is no maximum).

min_samples_leaf (int, default = 1)
Just as for a normal tree, this is the minimum number of samples each leaf has to contain. A low value will allow the tree to grow further, resulting (most likely) in a better accuracy on the training dataset at the expense of a risk of overfitting.

min_samples_split (int, default = 1)
Just as for a normal tree, this is the minimum number of samples a node has to contain to be split. Just as for the `min_samples_leaf` above, a low value will most likely result in a higher accuracy on the training set but might not improve the test set, or even harm it. Typically, a good k-fold cross-validation will help us determine the right trade-off between too deep and too shallow.

n_estimators (int, default = 10)
This is simply the number of trees in the forest. The higher, the better; at the expense of a longer computation time. At some point, the extra running time will not be worth the incremental minimal improvement.

criterion (string, default = "mse")
This is the KPI that the algorithm will minimize. Choose `mse` to optimize MSE or `mae` for MAE. As we discussed for the tree, the algorithm to create a random forest will take a much longer time to optimize itself for MAE instead of MSE.

Optimization

Just as for a single tree, we will optimize our random forest via a random search and a k-fold cross-validation. As you will see, the code is similar to the one that we used to optimize our regression tree. Note that we won't optimize the number of trees in our forest (`n_estimators`) for now, we will discuss this later on page 140.

```
from sklearn.ensemble import RandomForestRegressor
from sklearn.model_selection import RandomizedSearchCV

max_features = range(3,8)
max_depth = range(6,11)
min_samples_split = range(5,15)
min_samples_leaf = range(5,15)
bootstrap = [True,False]
```

Do It Yourself

```
10  param_dist = {'max_features': max_features,
11                'max_depth': max_depth,
12                'min_samples_split': min_samples_split,
13                'min_samples_leaf': min_samples_leaf,
14                'bootstrap': bootstrap}
15
16  forest = RandomForestRegressor(n_estimators=50, n_jobs=1)
17  forest_cv = RandomizedSearchCV(forest, param_dist, cv=6, n_jobs=-1,
        verbose=2, n_iter=400, scoring="neg_mean_absolute_error")
18  forest_cv.fit(X_train,Y_train)
```

Once this is done, we can print the optimal parameters and the accuracy achieved by our brand-new model.

```
1  print("Tuned Forest Parameters:", forest_cv.best_params_)
2
3  Y_train_pred = forest_cv.predict(X_train)
4  MAE_train = np.mean(abs(Y_train - Y_train_pred))/np.mean(Y_train)
5  print("Forest on training set MAE%:",round(MAE_train*100,1))
6
7  Y_test_pred = forest_cv.predict(X_test)
8  MAE_test = np.mean(abs(Y_test - Y_test_pred))/np.mean(Y_test)
9  print("Forest on test set MAE%:",round(MAE_test*100,1))
```

You should have something similar to:

```
1  Tuned Forest Parameters: {'min_samples_split': 10, 'min_samples_leaf': 7, '
      max_features': 6, 'max_depth': 9, 'bootstrap': True}
2  Forest on training set MAE%: 13.6
3  Forest on test set MAE%: 17.6
```

Keep in mind that the forests are random and therefore you will get (slightly) different results each time you run your model. On top of this, a random search does not test all the possible parameter combinations (that would take too much time!), so that you might get a different set of parameters.

Insights

Differences compared to a single tree

See how the optimal `max_depth` changed from the original optimal *lonely* tree from chapter 13 (it was 7) to the optimal tree in our (random) forest (it is now 9). The trees in the forest are now deeper. These deeper trees are more prone to overfitting, but the forest compensates this by the number of trees and the feature limitation (4 in our example). With less features to choose from at each node, our model will simply have to ask more questions to get to a proper forecast.

Number of trees in the forest

In order to save some computation time of our random search, we reduced the number of trees (`n_estimators`) in the forest to 30. Typically, the first parameter that you will want to increase to improve the accuracy of your forest is the number of trees. The more, the better. Of course, we could input a very high number, but that would come at the cost of computation time and wouldn't provide so much extra accuracy as of a certain number of trees. **There is a trade-off to be made between computation time and forecast accuracy**. The best way to know until when it is worth increasing the amount of trees is to plot the model accuracy based on the amount of trees.

Remember we are data scientists: we experiment.

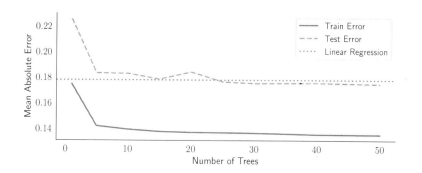

As you can see, as of around 30 trees, the incremental accuracy for any new tree is limited. But it seems, nevertheless, that the error decreases (very) slightly over time.

Insights

In order to get the best out of our forest – without increasing computation time too much neither – let's run a forest with our new optimal parameters and `n_estimators=200`. We can easily allow ourselves 200 trees on this dataset thanks to its limited size.

```
forest = RandomForestRegressor(n_estimators=200, min_samples_split=10,
    min_samples_leaf=7, max_features=6, max_depth=9, bootstrap=True)
forest.fit(X_train,Y_train)

Y_train_pred = forest.predict(X_train)
MAE_train = np.mean(abs(Y_train - Y_train_pred))/np.mean(Y_train)
print("Forest on training set MAE%:",round(MAE_train*100,1))

Y_test_pred = forest.predict(X_test)
MAE_test = np.mean(abs(Y_test - Y_test_pred))/np.mean(Y_test)
print("Forest on test set MAE%:",round(MAE_test*100,1))
```

And this is what we get:

```
Forest on training set MAE%: 13.5
Forest on test set MAE%: 17.5
```

As you can see, the accuracy improved only by 0.1% compared to the forest with 50 trees. Anyway, we are very happy as our forest is now beating the linear regression.

	Training	Test
Regression	17.8	17.8
Tree	17.1	19.8
Forest	13.5	17.5

So, can we improve our forecast further?

Yes, we can.

Chapter 16

Feature Importance

Statistical models are interesting as they can show us the interactions between the different input variables and the output. **Such models are easy to understand and to interpret**. In the first part of the book, we worked with many different exponential smoothing models: we could analyze them by simply looking at their level, trend or seasonality over time. Thanks to them, we can easily answer questions such as *Do we have a seasonality?* or *Is there a trend?*. And if the forecast for a specific period is strange, we can look how the sub-components (level, trend, seasonality) are behaving to understand where the error comes from.

It is unfortunately not the case with machine learning. These models are (very) difficult to interpret. A forest will never give you an estimation of the level, trend and seasonality of a product. You won't even know if the model *sees* a seasonality or a trend. Nevertheless, we have one tool at our disposal to understand how our machine learning algorithm thinks: the feature importances.

As you remember, we created a machine learning algorithm that looks at the last 12 months of historical car sales in Norway to predict the sales in the following month. In order to do that, we trained our model by showing it many different sequences of 13 months so that it could learn from these sequences how to predict the 13th month based on the 12 previous ones.

Before we continue with new models and further optimization, let's discuss the importance of these inputs. We do not know yet which of these 12 historical months is the most important to predict the sales of the 13th.

We would like to answer questions such as:

- Is M-1 more important than M-12?
- Is M-5 of any help?

When we grow a tree or a forest, we can get an idea of each feature's[1] importance. There are different definitions and ways to compute each feature's importance; we will focus on the one used by the scikit-learn library. Basically, the importance of a feature is the reduction it brings to the objective the algorithm tries to minimize. In our case, we want to bring the MAE or the RMSE down, therefore the feature importance is measured as the forecast accuracy each feature brings. The feature importance is then normalized so that its sum over all features is 1.

Before we discuss the implementation in Python, let's plot the feature importance we get from our random forest. Data visualization is a very important part of any data science project.

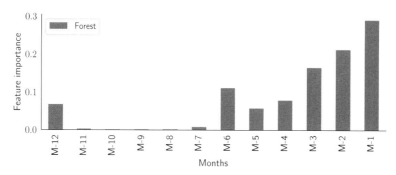

Figure 16.1: Feature importance

As we can see on figure 16.1, the recent months (M-1 to M-3) are very important (more than half of the total information comes from these 3 months) to forecast M+1. We then have 2 relatively helpful months: M-12 (the is the same month as M+1 but on Y-1) and M-6 (maybe used to check if there is a seasonality, as this month is at the exact opposite of the calendar). The other months (M-11 to M-7) are virtually useless.

Feature importance will be a useful technique to prevent our model from overfitting, as we are now able to see which feature brings an added value or not. We will discuss this further in chapter 14, when we optimize the number of historical months our model will use to make a forecast, and in chapter 20, when we add external information to our model.

---

[1]In our case, each feature is one of the 12 previous periods.

Do It Yourself

As a general piece of advice, do not hesitate to plot the feature importance of any new model you create. If you see that some features have a very limited importance, try to exclude them. This might make your model faster and more precise (as it will have a limited risk of overfitting).

Do It Yourself

Let's create the code to make a feature importance graph like figure 16.1. We start by creating a list (features) that will contain each feature name.

```
features = []
columns = X_train.shape[1]
for column in range(columns):
    features.append("M-"+str(columns-column))
```

We can then extract the feature importance from our forest model thanks to its attribute feature_importances_ and reshape this to a vertical array (thanks to reshape(-1,1)).

```
imp_forest = forest.feature_importances_.reshape(-1,1)
```

We can then save these features and their respective importance into a DataFrame.

```
importances = pd.DataFrame(data=imp_forest,index=features,columns=["Forest"])
```

Finally, we can simply plot it and obtain a figure such as 16.1.

```
importances.plot(kind="bar")
```

Chapter 17

Extremely Randomized Trees

The idea behind the random forest was that we could obtain a better forecast accuracy by taking the average prediction of many different trees. To obtain different trees, we used two tricks that allowed us to create various slightly different trees from the same initial training dataset. The first trick was to limit the number of features the algorithm could choose from at each node split. The second trick was to create different random subsets of the initial training dataset (thanks to bootstrapping).

In 2006, Belgian researchers Pierre Geurts, Damien Ernst and Louis Wehenkel published a paper "Extremely randomized trees" [5] which introduced a third idea to further increase the differences between each tree. At each node, the algorithm will now choose a split point at random for each feature and then select the best split among these. That means that for our Norwegian car sales dataset, this new method will draw at each node 1 random split point for each of the 12 previous months (our features) and will choose among these 12 potential splits the best one to split the node.

The extremely randomized trees can also benefit from the bootstrapped dataset and feature limitation.

Speed

Another advantage compared to a regular random forest is the training speed of the extremely randomized trees algorithm (or Extra Trees Regressor – ETR as called by `scikit-learn`) vs the forest model. As you can see on figure 17.1, it is actually much faster than the random forest: it is 3 to 4 times faster than the forest on average on this dataset. This is due to the fact that this model goes faster to choose the split at each node as it only has a few possibilities.

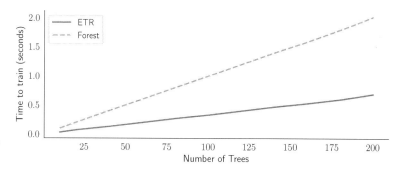

Figure 17.1: ETR vs Forest training time

But is the ETR model as accurate as the forest? The fact that it draws split points at random seems counter-intuitive, let's test it on our dataset!

Do It Yourself

We will once again use the `scikit-learn` library so that our code will be very similar to the one for the random forest.

```
from sklearn.ensemble import ExtraTreesRegressor

ETR = ExtraTreesRegressor(n_estimators=200, min_samples_split=10,
    min_samples_leaf=7, max_features=6, max_depth=9, bootstrap=True)

ETR.fit(X_train,Y_train)
```

The input parameters we use (`n_jobs`, `n_estimators`, `max_depth`, `max_features`, `min_samples_leaf`, `min_samples_split`) are the same as for the random forest.

Do It Yourself

Let's print the results

```
Y_train_pred = ETR.predict(X_train)
MAE_train = np.mean(abs(Y_train - Y_train_pred))/np.mean(Y_train)
print("ETR on training set MAE%:",round(MAE_train*100,1))

Y_test_pred = ETR.predict(X_test)
MAE_test = np.mean(abs(Y_test - Y_test_pred))/np.mean(Y_test)
print("ETR on test set MAE%:",round(MAE_test*100,1))
```

```
ETR on training set MAE%: 16.9
ETR on test set MAE%: 18.5
```

The results we obtain are less good than the ones we had with the forest (17.5% on the test set). Our previous forest parameters seem not to be appropriate for our new ETR model. Let's optimize these parameters.

Optimization

As for the random forest, we could be tempted to increase the number of trees to improve the accuracy over the test set; but as shown on figure 17.2, as of around 30 trees, the impact will be limited. In theory, ETR should benefit slightly more than the forest from an increased number of trees, as the ETR trees are more different from each others. The way to go to improve the accuracy further is actually to optimize the parameter via a random search.

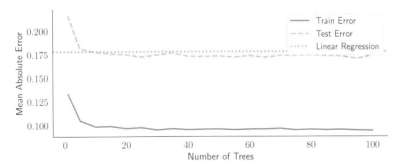

Figure 17.2: Impact of number of trees for the Extremely Randomized Trees model

We will do a random search on our ETR model just as we did for our forest.

```
from sklearn.ensemble import ExtraTreesRegressor
from sklearn.model_selection import RandomizedSearchCV

max_features = range(6,11)
max_depth = range(8,15)
min_samples_split = range(2,10,2)
min_samples_leaf = range(2,10,2)
bootstrap = [True,False]

param_dist = {'max_features': max_features,
              'max_depth': max_depth,
              'min_samples_split': min_samples_split,
              'min_samples_leaf': min_samples_leaf,
              'bootstrap': bootstrap}

ETR = ExtraTreesRegressor(n_estimators=200, n_jobs=1)
ETR_cv = RandomizedSearchCV(ETR, param_dist, cv=5, verbose=5, n_jobs=-1, n_iter=300, scoring="neg_mean_absolute_error")
ETR_cv.fit(X_train,Y_train)
```

We can now show the optimal parameters and compute the accuracy they achieved.

```
print("Tuned ETR Parameters:",ETR_cv.best_params_)

Y_train_pred = ETR_cv.predict(X_train)
MAE_train = np.mean(abs(Y_train - Y_train_pred))/np.mean(Y_train)
print("ETR on training set MAE%:",round(MAE_train*100,1))

Y_test_pred = ETR_cv.predict(X_test)
MAE_test = np.mean(abs(Y_test - Y_test_pred))/np.mean(Y_test)
print("ETR on test set MAE%:",round(MAE_test*100,1))
```

You should obtain something similar to

```
Tuned ETR Parameters: {'min_samples_split': 2, 'min_samples_leaf': 2, 'max_features': 10, 'max_depth': 11, 'bootstrap': False}
ETR on training set MAE%: 9.5
ETR on test set MAE%: 17.3
```

Randomness As for the forest, the results of an ETR are slightly random. This means that you might get different MAEs if you run this

Do It Yourself

experiment on your computer. Remember that the random search is also random as it does not test all the parameter possibilities (and uses random k-fold subsets). This means that running twice the random search for the ETR might give you slightly different parameter sets.

Differences compared to the forest As you can see, the maximum number of features came from 6 with the forest to 10 with the ETR. This is expected as the ETR cannot choose the optimal split point for each feature, instead it has to deal with random split points. As the split points are random, the risk of overfitting is lower so that, the ETR can use more features at once compared to the forest.

We now obtain an MAE% on the test set of 17.3%, which is better than the 17.8 obtained via the linear regression and also better than the 17.5% obtained via the forest.

	Training	Test
Regression	17.8	17.8
Tree	16.8	18.1
Forest	13.5	17.5
ETR	9.5	17.3

ETR is often better than a forest and always faster. **This model is both reliable and fast**, do not hesitate to use it as your first go-to model for any new project.

As always, the question is, can we improve our model further?

Chapter 18

Feature Optimization

> *The more you know about the past, the better you are prepared for the future.*
> Theodore Roosevelt

So far, we have created three different models (a regression tree, a random forest, and a set of extremely randomized trees), and we optimized each of them via a random search to automatically run through possible parameter sets that we test via a k-fold cross-validation.

We took the time to choose a model and we took the time to optimize its parameters. There is one thing that we haven't optimized (yet): the dataset itself.

The different models we used so far have a very interesting feature: once fitted to a training dataset, they can show each input's (i.e. feature) importance. Remember that, in our case, the input features are the different historical periods we use to populate our forecast. For our car sales in Norway, we used the last 12 months of sales to predict the next month: these are our features. We previously looked at the feature importance of our random forest and saw that M-1 was the most important month, leaving half of the other months useless. As you can see on figure 18.1, if we do the same exercise with the extra trees model, we obtain a much flatter curve.

How can we explain this? As you might remember, the difference between the extra trees model and the random forest lies into the fact that the split point that is chosen at each node is not the optimal one but can only be chosen among a set of random points for each selected feature. So that even though M-1 should be the most useful feature, in many cases,

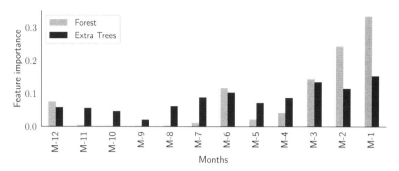

Figure 18.1: Feature importance

the random split point proposed for this feature is not the best across the different possibilities the algorithm can choose from.

Based on this graph, we can then ask ourselves an important question: *what if we used 13 months instead of 12 to make a forecast?* To answer this question, we will have to do a lot of experiments (on our training set).

First experiment – training set

The first experiment we will perform will consist of running our forest and our extra trees model on a training set based on 6 to 50 months and plot the results. You can see them on figure 18.2

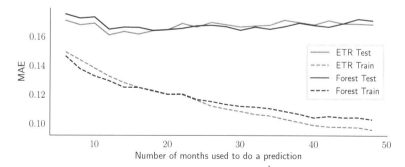

Figure 18.2: Feature Optimization

We see on this graph that, as we increase the number of months the model takes into account to make a prediction, the error over the training set

First experiment – training set

is reduced. This effect only seems to slow down at around 40 months for the forest and seems to continue for the extra trees. We actually have two effects here:

1. More input features allow our model to learn more patterns from the noise of the training set (as we discussed in chapter 8). This drives the error down. But only on the training set unfortunately. **This is pure overfitting**.
2. More input features also means less data available, as we cannot make as many loops through the original dataset as before (as we discussed in chapter 12). This will increase the test set error as the model has less data to learn from. **As there is less data in the training set, it is also easier for the model to overfit it**. Fortunately, this Norwegian car sales dataset is very long. We have nearly 10 years of history. So this effect is actually rather limited for us, on this specific example. Pay attention that it might not be the case on another dataset. Shorter historical datasets (3 to 5 years) will suffer a lot from this.

Note that both effects will drive the overfitting up, as we have at the same time less data to train on and more input features to learn from. And this is what we observe on figure 18.2: we clearly see that even as the training error is reduced over and over as we increase the number of features, the error on the test set seems to decrease until around 14-16 months and then increase slowly. This means that as of a certain number of input features, our model will not learn anything meaningful anymore and just overfit the training set.

What should we do then? Could we just look at the results over the test set and take from there the optimal number of months we should take into account?

No, we cannot. We would be overfitting the test set. Don't do this. Remember that the test set should only be used to note the final accuracy we obtained on fully unseen data. If we used the test set to choose the optimal parameter set, we would generate some really good results today that we would not be sure to be able to replicate tomorrow. This is very bad as we would be relying on luck to achieve the same results on new data and – based on these excellent results – we would be overcommiting our model.

The experiment we designed simply does not give us the appropriate answer to our initial question: *how many months should we take into account?* We will have to design a new one. But first, let's see how we can implement this first technique.

Do It Yourself

We will create a loop that runs our two models – Forest & ETR – for each possible x_len and measure their accuracy on both the training set and the test set. Let's divide this into multiple steps.

First, we will define the parameters we want to have for both the Forest (forest_features) and the ETR (ETR_features). As well as the range of historical horizons (n_months) we want to investigate. We will also create a list (results) to record our results.

```
from sklearn.ensemble import RandomForestRegressor
from sklearn.ensemble import ExtraTreesRegressor
import pandas as pd
import numpy as np

forest_features = {"n_jobs":-1,"n_estimators":100, "max_features":0.3, "bootstrap":False, "max_depth":9, "min_samples_split":12, "min_samples_leaf":8}
ETR_features = {"n_jobs":-1, "n_estimators":100, "max_features":0.9, "bootstrap":False, "max_depth":10, "min_samples_split":7, "min_samples_leaf":4}

n_months = range(6,50,2)
results = []
```

We have defined forest_features and ETR_features as two dictionaries. Actually, in Python, you can pass multiple arguments to a function at once by passing a dictionary. Passing **dict to a function means that you will pass each key-value pair of the dictionary as separate arguments to the function. Basically,

```
function("a"=1,"b"=2)
```

is the same as

```
dict = {"a":1,"b":2}
function(**dict)
```

That means that we will be able to call our models with all our features simply by typing

First experiment – training set

```
ETR = ExtraTreesRegressor(**ETR_features)
```

This is very convenient as we can define our parameters at the top of our code, in a dictionary, and then pass them all at once when needed in the loop.

We are now ready to loop through all the possible historical horizons.

```
for x_len in n_months: # We loop through the different x_len

    X_train, Y_train, X_test, Y_test = datasets(df, x_len=x_len)

    forest = RandomForestRegressor(**forest_features)
    ETR = ExtraTreesRegressor(**ETR_features)
    models = [("Forest",forest), ("ETR",ETR)]

    for name,model in models: # We loop through the models

        model.fit(X_train,Y_train)
        Y_train_pred = model.predict(X_train)
        mae_train = np.mean(abs(Y_train - Y_train_pred))/np.mean(Y_train
            )
        Y_test_pred = model.predict(X_test)
        mae_test = np.mean(abs(Y_test - Y_test_pred))/np.mean(Y_test)

        results.append([name+" Train",mae_train,x_len])
        results.append([name+" Test",mae_test,x_len])
```

We now have a `list results` that contains all our results. Let's format it a bit so that we can make a figure similar to 18.2.

```
data = pd.DataFrame(results,columns=["Model","MAE%","Number of
    Months"])
data = data.set_index(["Number of Months","Model"]).stack().unstack("
    Model")
data.index = data.index.droplevel(level=1)
data.index.name = "Number of months"
```

We can then simply plot `data` thanks to the method `.plot()` to obtain something similar to figure 18.2.

```
data.plot(color=["orange"]*2+["black"]*2,style=["-","--"]*2)
```

You can also populate a summary table with the optimal number of months that was obtained on each dataset thanks to one line of code.

```
1  print(data.idxmin())
```

Second experiment – validation set

We saw that our first experiment didn't give us the result we wanted as our model overfitted the training set; so that the error on the training set did not give us any meaningful information about the expected error on the test set. In chapter 14, we saw that we could use the k-fold cross-validation method to properly test each parameter set. The idea was to cut the training set into n subsets and run n trials with each time one of these subsets kept as a validation set. The final error would then be the average of the error obtained over each validation set. Let's do the same here and run for each different possible number of features n different trials with each time a different validation set.

You can see on figure 18.3 the accuracy we obtain on the validation set.

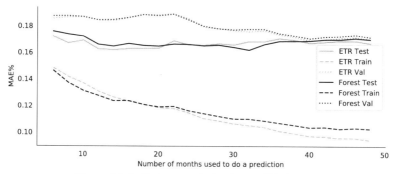

Figure 18.3: Feature optimization: validation set

These results are already much better! The accuracy obtained on the validation set is much more aligned with the one obtained on the test set compared to what we obtained with the training set. Nevertheless, if we look at the optimal number of input features (see table 18.1), we see that the optimal number of months is fairly different for the validation set (around 40 months) and the test set (around 12–18!).

Second experiment – validation set

	ETR	Forest
Train	48	48
Validation	42	48
Test	12	18

Table 18.1: Optimal results

We observe some interesting behaviours:

1. We have to use a rather high number of k-folds (8 in the example) to reduce the result's randomness (due to the variability of each subset). A higher number of k-folds will also limit the reduced amount of data available for our model to learn from. With 8 k-folds, the model only loses 12.5% of its training dataset; which is already a small penalty. On the other hand, as we use more k-folds, the computation time explodes.
2. The initial error of the validation set is higher than the one of the test set. This can be explained as the test set is a rather "easy" dataset. We know this thanks to the regression we used as a benchmark, which obtained a better score on the test set than on the training set.
3. As we use more and more months to make our prediction, the error on the validation set goes down and the error on the test set grows bigger. Until they cross at around 40 months.

This last point is rather interesting: how come the validation error seems to shrink with a higher number of months whereas the test set error grows?

A possible explanation comes, maybe, from the fact that each year is a bit different. In a typical business, you might face some unusual years. Maybe January last year was really good or you had an issue in April. These can be due to new legislation, new competitors – or the bankruptcy of some others – the introduction of a breakthrough new product, etc. As our machine learning models get more and more input features, they start to remember these small bumps in the demand. As the validation set is composed of random extracts of the training dataset, it contains years that the model knows already. So that the model doesn't just predict *a* month but recognizes that we want it to predict April 2015, which was 5% higher than usual. Somehow, the model is overfitting the validation set, as it learns historical patterns that won't happen again in the future.

Once again, we will have to find a new experiment method to overcome this overfitting. But first, let's take a look at how you can implement this technique.

Do It Yourself

We will use the `KFold` function from the `scikit-learn` library. This will allow us to randomly cut our training dataset into a validation set and a new training set. In our code, we will create `kf` as an instance of a `KFold` object (see line 11). It will be used to cut our training dataset into 8 splits.

```
from sklearn.model_selection import KFold

for x_len in n_months:

    X_train, Y_train, X_test, Y_test = datasets(df, x_len=x_len)

    forest = RandomForestRegressor(**forest_features)
    ETR = ExtraTreesRegressor(**ETR_features)
    models = [("Forest",forest), ("ETR",ETR)]

    kf = KFold(n_splits=8)

    for name,model in models:

        mae_kfold_train = []
        mae_kfold_val = []

        for train_index, val_index in kf.split(X_train):

            X_train_kfold, X_val_kfold = X_train[train_index], X_train[val_index]
            Y_train_kfold, Y_val_kfold = Y_train[train_index], Y_train[val_index]

            model.fit(X_train_kfold,Y_train_kfold)
            Y_train_pred = model.predict(X_train_kfold)
            mae_kfold_train.append(np.mean(abs(Y_train_kfold - Y_train_pred))/
                np.mean(Y_train_kfold))
            Y_val_pred = model.predict(X_val_kfold)
            mae_kfold_val.append(np.mean(abs(Y_val_kfold - Y_val_pred))/np.
                mean(Y_val_kfold))

        model.fit(X_train,Y_train)
        Y_test_pred = model.predict(X_test)
        mae_test = np.mean(abs(Y_test - Y_test_pred))/np.mean(Y_test)

        results.append([name+" Val",np.mean(mae_kfold_val),x_len])
        results.append([name+" Train",np.mean(mae_kfold_train),x_len])
        results.append([name+" Test",mae_test,x_len])
```

Like for the first experiment, we can also clean our `DataFrame results` in order to plot it.

```
data = pd.DataFrame(results,columns=["Model","MAE%","Number of
    Months"])
data = data.set_index(["Number of Months","Model"]).stack().unstack("
    Model")
data.index = data.index.droplevel(level=1)
data.index.name = "Number of months"

print(data.idxmin())

data.plot(color=["orange"]*3+["black"]*3,style=["-","--",":"]*2)
```

Your plot will be similar to figure 18.3.

Third experiment – Holdout dataset

As we saw in our previous experiments, despite our best efforts with a powerful k-fold method, our model could overfit the validation set itself. We have to think of a smarter way to find the best model.

Why do we use a test set in the first place? The initial idea behind the test set is to keep a set of data aside so that we can run our model (once we have chosen one and optimized it) against it as it was real unseen data. On our example dataset, we kept the last 12 months as the test set (February 2016 to January 2017). We took the implicit assumption that the accuracy we would obtain on this 2016–2017 period would be similar to the accuracy we would achieve on a future forecast made for the remaining part of 2017 (assuming we would today be somewhere in February 2017).

A second test set? A smart new method is to create a second test set (based on 2015 for example) and keep the best model based on the 2015 results. We would somehow create a *pre* test set. We can then assume that the model that achieves the best results over 2015 would also perform well against 2016 and in the future as well. We will call this new test set the **holdout dataset**.

Results

On figure 18.4, you can see the results we obtain if we use a holdout dataset for each iteration of our models.

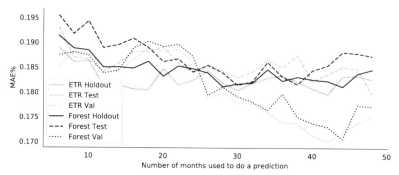

Figure 18.4: Results with holdout dataset

We observe two main behaviours:

1. The error on the validation set seems to decrease as the number of months increase.
2. The actual very good news is that the overall accuracy obtained on the holdout dataset behaves more or less the same as the one obtained on the test set.

	ETR	Forest
Train	48	48
Validation	44	44
Holdout	30	28
Test	40	24

Table 18.2: Optimal results

First observe, then conclude

As you might have noticed, the results shown on tables 18.1 (page 159) and 18.2 do not match exactly. This is normal, as the results vary from one simulation to another: both models contain a part of randomness and the validation set is also random (even if done based on 8 folds). One way to reduce randomness would be to increase the number of trees in both models, but that would come at the expense of computation time. Also as 2015 is not the same as 2016 (i.e. our test and holdout sets are not the same) the optimum on one of these two can be different from the optimum on the other one.

The initial question we asked ourselves was *"How many months should we take into account to do a prediction?"* and even though we found a good method to answer the question, the answer does not seem black or white due to all this randomness. It will often be the case with machine learning. That means that we cannot find a definitive answer to our simple question, but we can nevertheless draw some trends and refine the search space from these first trends. It will take a few iterations to come to very good results. But – due to the randomness – you will unfortunately never select a **perfect** model.

The best model for 2015 might not be the best one for 2016, which might not be the best one for 2017. And so on. It is therefore important to understand that we should not draw definitive conclusions by saying that as one set of parameters is the best for 2015, it will also be the best in the future. What if we were just lucky?

Back to feature importance

A careful observation of the results and the main trends, as well as some experience in modeling, might help us to a find a **very good** model – which might not be the **best** model on this holdout dataset. In order to do this analysis, let's plot on figure 18.5 the different feature importances if we create a model with 26 months.

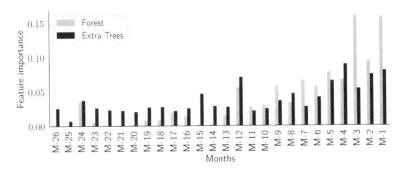

Figure 18.5: Feature importance for 26 months

We are looking here for patterns rather than definitive direct conclusions. We observe that,

1. the first year (months M-1 to M-12) is much more important than the second;
2. the very first months of -Y2 and -Y3 (M-13 and M-25) are nearly useless;
3. M-12 and M-24 seem to be more important that the months just next to them. This is normal: we only want to predict one month in the future and these are the same month one and two years ago. Basically, if we want to forecast January 2017, these are January 2016 and 2015.

Based on these observations, we can restrict the number of possible models to either 12 or 24 months. Remember that, initially, the parameters we used for our models where given by a random search we did for models with 12 months. That means that the models with 24 months might be better with a (slightly) different set of parameters.

Finally, in order to decide to use either one or two years of input data, we should launch a new random search on the models that take 24 months as an input for them to be optimized as well. We should then use the results of these models against a holdout set to determine if we want to keep a forest and an ETR with 12 or 24 months.

That is a lot of work, but careful optimization has a cost. Hopefully Python will allow us to automate most of this.

It is very important to note here that the conclusion we drew for this dataset might not apply to your dataset. But the process and the logic of the search will still be applicable. Also this conclusion holds true for a prediction only at M+1. It might be that if you want to create predictions at M+6, you might need to keep 18 months instead of 12 months. Machine learning feature optimization calls for many experiments.

Recap

Thanks to our holdout dataset, we could finally create an experiment that behaved similarly to the test set. Based on a first broad search, we could restrict the potential number of months we should use as an input. We then investigated in depth these few possibilities before choosing the best one.

Do It Yourself

We first have to redefine our **datasets** function (see page 118) for it to populate a holdout subset. **datasets** will now take as an input **holdout**, which is the number of periods we will keep aside on the holdout dataset (see lines 14–20).

```python
def datasets(df, x_len=12, y_len=1, y_test_len=12, holdout=0):

    D = df.values
    periods = D.shape[1]

    # Training set creation: run through all the possible time windows
    loops = periods + 1 - x_len - y_len - y_test_len
    train = []
    for col in range(loops):
        train.append(D[:,col:col+x_len+y_len])
    train = np.vstack(train)
    X_train, Y_train = np.split(train,[x_len],axis=1)

    rows = df.shape[0]
    if holdout > 0:
        X_train, X_holdout = np.split(X_train,[-rows*holdout],axis=0)
        Y_train, Y_holdout = np.split(Y_train,[-rows*holdout],axis=0)
    else:
        X_holdout = np.array([])
        Y_holdout = np.array([])

    # Test set creation: unseen "future" data with the demand just before
    max_col_test = periods - x_len - y_len + 1
    test = []
    for col in range(loops,max_col_test):
        test.append(D[:,col:col+x_len+y_len])
    test = np.vstack(test)
    X_test, Y_test = np.split(test,[x_len],axis=1)

    # this data formatting is needed if we only predict a single period
    if y_len == 1:
        Y_train = Y_train.ravel()
        Y_test = Y_test.ravel()
        Y_holdout = Y_holdout.ravel()

    return X_train, Y_train, X_holdout, Y_holdout, X_test, Y_test
```

We can now use this new function in our main loop (we will take the same structure as previously).

```
for x_len in n_months:

    X_train, Y_train, X_holdout, Y_holdout, X_test, Y_test = datasets(df, x_len=
        x_len, holdout=12)

    forest = RandomForestRegressor(**forest_features)
    ETR = ExtraTreesRegressor(**ETR_features)
    models = [("Forest",forest), ("ETR",ETR)]

    for name,model in models:

        model.fit(X_train,Y_train)
        Y_train_pred = model.predict(X_train)
        mae_train = np.mean(abs(Y_train - Y_train_pred))/np.mean(Y_train)
        Y_test_pred = model.predict(X_test)
        mae_test = np.mean(abs(Y_test - Y_test_pred))/np.mean(Y_test)
        Y_holdout_pred = model.predict(X_holdout)
        mae_holdout = np.mean(abs(Y_holdout - Y_holdout_pred))/np.mean(
            Y_holdout)

        results.append([name+" Train",mae_train,x_len])
        results.append([name+" Test",mae_test,x_len])
        results.append([name+" Holdout",mae_holdout,x_len])
```

We can of course plot the results.

```
data = pd.DataFrame(results,columns=["Model","MAE%","Number of
    Months"])
data = data.set_index(["Number of Months","Model"]).stack().unstack("
    Model")
data.index = data.index.droplevel(level=1)
data.index.name = "Number of months"

print(data.idxmin())

data.plot(color=["orange"]*3+["black"]*3,style=["-","--",":"]*3)
```

Your plot will be similar to figure 18.4.

Chapter 19

Adaptive Boosting

We saw in chapters 15 and 17 two models – the forest and the extremely random trees – that both created a very good prediction by averaging many slightly different good models. These models are called *ensemble* models as they use an ensemble of different good models to make a prediction.

In 1997, Yoav Freund and Robert E. Schapire proposed a new approach in their paper "A Decision-Theoretic Generalization of On-Line Learning and an Application to Boosting" [2]. Their idea was to create a *boosting* model.

Their idea is based on the fact that it is better to use 100 *complementary* models rather than to average 100 good but rather *similar*[1] models.

Ok, but how do we create complementary models?

Rather than to aggregate many different models, Freund and Schapire's idea was to run a first simple model (typically a very simple tree), see what it got wrong, then create a second one that puts more emphasis on the mistakes that the first model made, and so on. You can end up, for example, with a hundred trees built one after another, specialized each time on the previous tree's mistakes. In the end, you will not have 100 generalistic good models but rather 100 models that complement each other by each time focusing on the mistakes made by the previous models.

Their model is called **Adaptive Boosting** – or AdaBoost.

---

[1] Note that the ETR improved the forest model by creating less good but more different trees.

How does it work?

The AdaBoost algorithm will follow these steps

1. Generate a first *weak* model (i.e. a model that is slightly more accurate than luck – typically a very simple tree).
2. Compute the prediction error of the current model on the training set.
3. Update the training set by allocating a higher importance to the training samples that got the biggest prediction error.
4. Generate a new *weak* model that is trained on the updated training set. Note that the dataset used to train this new weak model is randomly generated (based on the original training set). Each sample has a certain probability to be included based on the importance computed on step 3.
5. Repeat steps 2-4 until a certain threshold is reached (for example a fixed number of trees) or the training error goes to... 0!
As you will see, an AdaBoost model can achieve a *perfect* prediction on the training set.

Insights

The AdaBoost algorithm implementation in `scikit-learn` only has three hyperparameters:

base_estimator this is the weak model we want to boost. Typically, we will use a tree with a specified `max_depth`.

n_estimators the number of weak models we will generate.

learning_rate the importance of each new weak model.

Let's discuss these new parameters one by one.

Number of estimators

Let's first play with the number of estimators we will use. Each extra estimator means that the model gets a new weak predictor that is going to be fitted on the model's current mistakes. Basically, that's an extra chance to get these mistakes right. As you can see on figure 19.1, the error on the training set keeps on decreasing as we throw more and more trees against it.

Insights

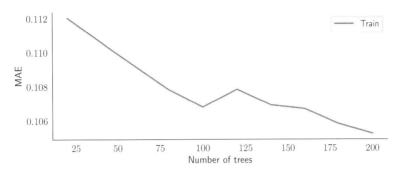

Figure 19.1: Adaboost vs training set

That's normal of course, as each new tree is fitted to compensate for the errors of the model. But what about the error on the test set? As you can see on figure 19.2, the test error does not follow the same curve (unfortunately). We actually see a significant decrease until around 60 trees. From there, the trend is less clear: it seems that 100 to 160 trees is a good number despite the bad results around 120 trees (maybe due to a lack of luck[1]).

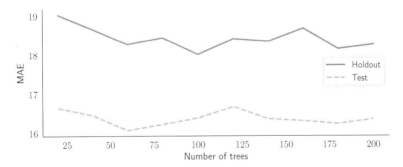

Figure 19.2: Adaboost vs test set

As we cannot rely on the training error to give meaningful indications, we will again use the holdout dataset (as defined on page 161) to analyze the accuracy of our model (and select the best parameters). We cannot directly use the results obtained against the test set to choose the best parameter set. That would definitely be overfitting.

---

[1] AdaBoost results are random as each new estimator gets a random selection of the updated dataset.

Speed

When we ran our forest and extra tree regressor, we could benefit from multi-processor computation (via the n_jobs parameter) as all the trees generated were independent from each other. One processor could work on the first tree as another processor would already be working on the second one. Unfortunately, this cannot happen with AdaBoost as each new tree is built based on the results of the previous tree. This means of course that the computation time for AdaBoost is going to be much longer than for a Forest or an ETR. Computation time is the first hurdle of AdaBoost.
Unfortunately, there are going to be two other ones.

Learning rate

The AdaBoost implementation allows us to apply a learning rate to each tree. When the model computes its prediction, this learning rate (which is a multiplicator) will be applied to the weight of each of the extra trees in order to decrease their weight in the final prediction. Of course, the learning rate does not impact the first tree of the model, which has a weight of 1^1. This learning rate is somehow a *shrinkage* effect applied to each extra tree's importance in the final prediction. Typical values range from 0.01 to 0.3.

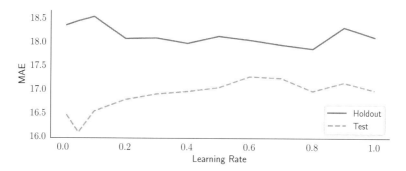

Figure 19.3: Learning rate impact

The learning rate is a good parameter to tackle the speed issue. The higher it is, the faster your model will evolve – but at the expense of a higher risk of overfitting. Generally speaking, it is always better to increase

---

[1]Applying the same weight to all the trees is like applying no weight at all.

Insights

the amount of estimators and to reduce the learning rate proportionally. This allows the model to get in a smooth way to a very good spot. Unfortunately, this will drive you into very long training time. A good technique would here be to set an arbitrary amount of trees (for example 100) that you are willing to train based on how slow/fast you want your model to be. Once you have decided the number of estimators you want, you can then search for the best estimator/learning rate!

Playing with trees

As said, an AdaBoost model only gets three parameters – the base estimator, the number of estimators and the learning rate – so that one could think that it is easy to find the best combination.
Unfortunately, nothing could be further from the truth.
The question of how we optimize the base estimator (a tree in our case) is as open as the optimization of a single tree on its own (as we did in chapter 14).

In order to simplify our supply chain data scientist lives, let's focus on one main parameter of a tree: the maximum depth it can have. You can see on figure 19.4 the results we obtain based on different maximum depths.

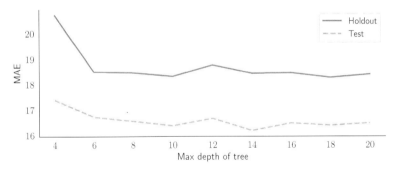

Figure 19.4: Maximum depth of the base estimator

As you can see, it seems that a maximum depth of 10 is a good value. Deeper trees wouldn't result in a significantly decreased error on the holdout set – or even a slight increase of the error. Generally speaking, as we use deeper trees, we face the risk that our model overfit the training set and apply erroneous patterns to predict the test set. We do not want this, especially as deeper trees are slower to run.

Do It Yourself

Simple model

Let's start with a simple code to run our first Adaptive Boosting model.

```
from sklearn.tree import DecisionTreeRegressor
from sklearn.ensemble import AdaBoostRegressor

ada = AdaBoostRegressor(DecisionTreeRegressor(max_depth=8),
    n_estimators=100, learning_rate=0.01)
ada = ada.fit(X_train,Y_train)
```

As usual, we can now measure the accuracy of our new model.

```
Y_train_pred = ada.predict(X_train)
MAE_train = np.mean(abs(Y_train - Y_train_pred))/np.mean(Y_train)
print("Ada on training set MAE%:",round(MAE_train*100,1))

Y_test_pred = ada.predict(X_test)
MAE_test = np.mean(abs(Y_test - Y_test_pred))/np.mean(Y_test)
print("Ada on test set MAE%:",round(MAE_test*100,1))
```

You should obtain something similar to

```
Ada on training set MAE%: 10.7
Ada on test set MAE%: 17.7
```

Parameter optimization

Unfortunately, our beloved `RandomizedSearchCV` function from `scikit-learn` won't allow us to run automatically through different regression tree designs (i.e. different maximum depths). We will have to loop through different tree designs and run for each a `RandomizedSearchCV`. We then have to select the tree design (i.e. the maximum depth) that gave the best result.

As we discussed, the accuracy obtained on the training set is irrelevant for a model such as AdaBoost. Therefore, we will have to use a holdout dataset to select the best parameter set among each possible maximum depth. We will use the `datasets` function that we created on page 165 to populate our `X_holdout` & `Y_holdout` datasets.

Do It Yourself

Before we go for our main loop, let's import all the libraries and create our main variables.

```
from sklearn.model_selection import RandomizedSearchCV
from sklearn.tree import DecisionTreeRegressor
from sklearn.ensemble import AdaBoostRegressor

X_train, Y_train, X_holdout, Y_holdout, X_test, Y_test = datasets(df, x_len
    =12, holdout=12)

n_estimators = [60,80,100,120,140]
learning_rate = [0.0001,0.0005,0.001,0.005,0.01]
param_dist = {"n_estimators": n_estimators,
              "learning_rate": learning_rate}

results = []
```

Let's go through our loop now! We will use the `list results` to store all our results along the way.

```
for max_depth in range(6,18,2):

    ada = AdaBoostRegressor(DecisionTreeRegressor(max_depth=
        max_depth))
    ada_cv = RandomizedSearchCV(ada, param_dist, n_jobs=-1, cv=5,
        n_iter=20, scoring="neg_mean_absolute_error")
    ada_cv.fit(X_train,Y_train)

    Y_train_pred = ada_cv.predict(X_train)
    Y_holdout_pred = ada_cv.predict(X_holdout)
    Y_test_pred = ada_cv.predict(X_test)

    print("Tuned AdaBoost Parameters:",ada_cv.best_params_)
    result_train = np.mean(abs(Y_train - Y_train_pred))/np.mean(Y_train)
    result_hold = np.mean(abs(Y_holdout - Y_holdout_pred))/np.mean(
        Y_holdout)
    result_test = np.mean(abs(Y_test - Y_test_pred))/np.mean(Y_test)

    results.append([result_train,result_hold,result_test,max_depth,ada_cv.
        best_params_])
```

The `results list` now holds the results of the best model that our random search could find for each maximum depth. We can transform `results` into a `DataFrame` and then simply print the parameter set that got the lowest error on the holdout set. In order to do this, we will call the method idxmin() on our DataFrame.

idxmin() returns the position of the lowest element in a DataFrame. It is the same as the NumPy function np.argmin() (that we already used on page 58).

```
results = pd.DataFrame(results)
results.columns = ["MAE Train","MAE Holdout","MAE Test","Max Depth","Best Params"]
best_results = results["MAE Holdout"].idxmin()
print(results.iloc[best_results])
```

let's take a look at the results!

```
MAE Train 0.101936
MAE Holdout 0.182019
MAE Test 0.18009
Max Depth 8
Best Params {'n_estimators': 140, 'learning_rate': 0.001}
```

These results might seem rather disappointing to you: it seems that the extra complexity of AdaBoost didn't pay-off on this dataset.

Nevertheless, we miss one step here: when we created our training and test sets, we left 12 months on the side for our holding set. Actually, we should now use all the historical period to populate our training set and retrain our model. Let's see what happens.

```
X_train, Y_train, X_holdout, Y_holdout, X_test, Y_test = datasets(df, x_len=12, holdout=0)
ada = AdaBoostRegressor(DecisionTreeRegressor(max_depth=10), n_estimators=100,learning_rate=0.0005)
ada = ada.fit(X_train,Y_train)

Y_train_pred = ada.predict(X_train)
MAE_train = np.mean(abs(Y_train - Y_train_pred))/np.mean(Y_train)
print("Ada on training set MAE%:",round(MAE_train*100,1))

Y_test_pred = ada.predict(X_test)
MAE_test = np.mean(abs(Y_test - Y_test_pred))/np.mean(Y_test)
print("Ada on test set MAE%:",round(MAE_test*100,1))
```

Do It Yourself

And this is what we obtain now:

```
Ada on training set MAE%: 10.7
Ada on test set MAE%: 16.6
```

That's much better than previously! As you can see, AdaBoost is data intensive and sensitive as only one year less of data resulted in a major difference of accuracy. This extra amount of data, fortunately, was enough for AdaBoost to beat our ETR model.

	Training	Test
Regression	17.8	17.8
Tree	16.8	18.1
Forest	13.5	17.5
ETR	9.5	17.3
AdaBoost	10.7	16.6

Is there any other way to decrease the error further? Yes of course! We still have some more ideas and models to discuss. But before, let's discuss how we can populate a forecast for multiple periods with AdaBoost.

Multiple periods

As we have discussed, AdaBoost is unfortunately slow and it doesn't have a straightforward way to do a randomized search. On top of that, its implementation in `scikit-learn` can only predict one single output at a time. This means that you can only fit your AdaBoost model to forecast one single period at a time. If you want to forecast multiple periods at once (i.e. Y_train & Y_test have multiple columns), you will have to cut these into sub-models to predict one period at a time.

Luckily, our friends from `scikit-learn` created a model wrapper `MultiOutputRegressor` which allows us to easily fit our AdaBoost model to predict multiple periods at once.

`MultiOutputRegressor` behaves like any `scikit-learn` model and takes two inputs:

> **estimator** This is the base estimator (i.e. our AdaBoost model) that we will use to predict multiple outputs
>
> **n_jobs** Just as for the Forest or the ETR model, we can now use multiple cores of our machine in parallel. As for all `scikit-learn`, n_jobs=-1 means that you want it to use all your machine's cores.

Actually, the function will dedicate one core to each period you want to predict. So that, even if you can't speed up the training of one AdaBoost model, you can train multiple different models at once. By using this, we will kill two birds with one stone, as we have now speeded up our training time and the ability to predict multiple periods at once.

```
from sklearn.ensemble import AdaBoostRegressor
from sklearn.tree import DecisionTreeRegressor
from sklearn.multioutput import MultiOutputRegressor

def AdaBoost_multi(X_train, Y_train, X_holdout, Y_holdout, X_test, Y_test):
    base_estimator = DecisionTreeRegressor(max_depth=6)
    ada = AdaBoostRegressor(base_estimator=base_estimator, n_estimators=100,
        learning_rate=0.025)

    multi = MultiOutputRegressor(ada,n_jobs=-1)
    multi.fit(X_train,Y_train)

    Y_train_pred = multi.predict(X_train)
    Y_holdout_pred = multi.predict(X_holdout)
    Y_test_pred = multi.predict(X_test)

    return Y_train_pred, Y_holdout_pred, Y_test_pred
```

Finally, we can simply run our model against our dataset.

```
X_train, Y_train, X_holdout, Y_holdout, X_test, Y_test = datasets(df, y_len
    =4,x_len=12, holdout=12)
Y_train_pred, Y_holdout_pred, Y_test_pred = AdaBoost_multi(X_train, Y_train
    , X_holdout, Y_holdout, X_test, Y_test)
```

Chapter 20

Exogenous Information & Leading Indicators

> *Felix, qui potuit rerum cognoscere causas.*
> Fortunate, who was able to know the causes of things.
> Virgil (70 - 19 BC)

Until now, we have made our forecasts solely on the basis of historical demand. We have discussed in chapter 14 how to optimize our model and we have discussed in chapter 18 how to optimize how many previous periods we should take into account to make a prediction. There is something we haven't discussed yet: which other factors could we be looking at to predict future demand?

For many businesses, the historical sales are actually not the only – nor the main – factor that drives future sales. Other internal and external factors drive the demand as well. You might sell more or less depending on the weather, the GDP growth, unemployment rate, loan rates and so on. These **external factors**[1] are often called **leading indicators**.

The demand can also be driven by some company decisions: price changes, promotions, marketing budget, another product's sales... As these factors result from business decisions, we will call them **internal factors**. We will group both internal and external factors into the term **exogenous factors** (as these factors are *exogenous* to the historical demand), as you can see on figure 20.1.

---

[1] External as a company does not control them.

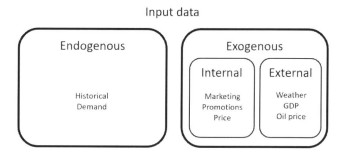

Figure 20.1: Input data classification

Linear regressions?

As we discussed in the previous chapters, one of the limitations of the different exponential smoothing models was their inability to deal with any of this exogenous information. Typically, in most of the trainings about forecast, this is when you will be shown linear regressions such as: "Our sales increase by 10% during weekends" or "Demand increases by 10% for every degree above 25". And you will be shown data where this works quite well. Like on figure 20.2.

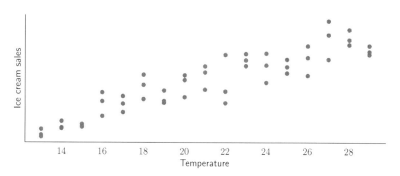

Figure 20.2: My sales are linearly correlated to temperature!

Unfortunately, this kind of relationships do not extend very well. Let's imagine that figure 20.2 was showing ice cream sales based on the daily temperature. We understand that if the temperature decreases, so will your sales. But will your sales shrink to zero if it is freezing? Will everyone stop eating ice cream? Maybe not. Will people start selling you back your ice cream if the temperature goes low enough? Most likely not.

Typically, as you can see on figure 20.3, the sales will flatten around a certain minimum as of a certain temperature.

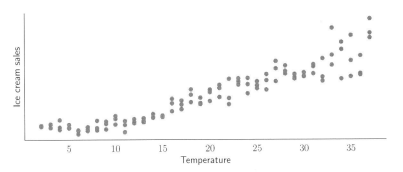

Figure 20.3: My sales are not so linearly correlated to temperature

We can actually ask ourselves many other questions:

- Is the temperature more impactful during the weekend or on Monday?
- Aren't the customers buying more ice cream if it has been hot for more than just one day straight?
- Do customers buy ice cream on Friday if they know that the weekend is going to be sunny?
- Do sales increase during holidays no matter what the temperature is?

Answering these questions via linear regressions would call for many different models. Yet, these models will only take into account temperature to predict sales and they totally ignore the historical demand level.

This is exactly where machine learning models will shine. They are very good at understanding these relationships, their limitations, and how they evolve depending on the different inputs.

Data preparation

Before we discuss how we will integrate these exogenous data into our historical demand dataset, let's first recap how we formatted our initial dataset in chapter 12.

We created a training set by looping through our historical demand (see table 20.1) using as an input n consecutive periods to predict m consecutive future periods.

Product	Y1				Y2				Y3			
	Q1	Q2	Q3	Q4	Q1	Q2	Q3	Q4	Q1	Q2	Q3	Q4
#1	5	15	10	7	6	13	11	5	4	11	9	4
#2	7	2	3	1	1	0	0	1	3	2	4	5
#3	18	25	32	47	56	70	64	68	72	67	65	58
#4	4	1	5	3	2	5	3	1	4	3	2	5

Table 20.1: Typical historical demand dataset

Table 20.2 shows you an example for $n = 4$ and $m = 1$.

Loop	Product	Y1				Y2				Y3			
		Q1	Q2	Q3	Q4	Q1	Q2	Q3	Q4	Q1	Q2	Q3	Q4
#1	#1	5	15	10	7	6							
#1	#2	7	2	3	1	1							
#1	#3	18	25	32	47	56							
#1	#4	4	1	5	3	2							
#2	#1		15	10	7	6	13						
#2	#2		2	3	1	1	0						
#2	#3		25	32	47	56	70						
#2	#4		1	5	3	2	5						
#3	#1			10	7	6	13	11					
...	...			...	...	...	...	...					

Table 20.2: Training set based on the historical dataset

Now let's add one leading indicator to this dataset, for example the GDP growth.

Product	Y1				Y2			
	Q1	Q2	Q3	Q4	Q1	Q2	Q3	Q4
GDP growth	1.0	0.9	1.2	1.3	2.5	2.1	2.6	2.7
#1	5	15	10	7	6	13	11	5
#2	7	2	3	1	1	0	0	1
#3	18	25	32	47	56	70	64	68
#4	4	1	5	3	2	5	3	1

How should we feed this GDP growth to our model? To answer this question, let's go one step back: *what is the relationship we want to have between GDP and our sales?* We assume that the GDP of a specific

Data preparation

quarter will have an impact on our sales. This means that to predict the sales of Y+1, you'll have to know the GDP of Y+1 (we don't want our tool to predict the GDP of Y+1!). When creating our training dataset, we'll systematically add to X_train the GDP growth over the historical periods but also over the future periods. This actually means that our model will be able to look, in order to make a forecast, at how the GDP growth behaved during the last four quarters, as well as how much it will be during the next quarter.

The process to create X_train and Y_train datasets will look like table 20.3.

Loop	Product	\multicolumn{4}{c|}{X_train Previous demand}	\multicolumn{4}{c|}{Previous GDP}	Future GDP	Y_train Future demand
#1	#1	5	15	10	7	1.0	0.9	1.2	1.3	2.5	6
#1	#2	7	2	3	1	1.0	0.9	1.2	1.3	2.5	1
#1	#3	18	25	32	47	1.0	0.9	1.2	1.3	2.5	56
#1	#4	4	1	5	3	1.0	0.9	1.2	1.3	2.5	2
#2	#1	15	10	7	6	0.9	1.2	1.3	2.5	2.1	13
...	...	...	...	...	...	...	...	...	...	...	...

Table 20.3: X_train & Y_train creation

So that our model will learn the relationship from table 20.4.

\multicolumn{9}{c}{X_train}	→	Y_train
5	15	10	7	1.0	0.9	1.2	1.3	2.5	→	6
7	2	3	1	1.0	0.9	1.2	1.3	2.5	→	1
18	25	32	47	1.0	0.9	1.2	1.3	2.5	→	56
4	1	5	3	1.0	0.9	1.2	1.3	2.5	→	2
15	10	7	6	0.9	1.2	1.3	2.5	2.1	→	13
...	...	...	...	...	...	...	...	...	→	...

Table 20.4: X_train & Y_train relationship

What might be counter-intuitive here is that it does not matter for our algorithm how we organize X_train. You can put first the future GDP, then the historical demand and finish with the previous GDP; it won't change a thing. You could even randomly shuffle all the columns. The model does not think like a human brain, it does not project a relationship from one column to the next one. So that it actually does not need to have any meaningful order in its inputs.

You can now simply use this training dataset directly into your favorite model.

Insights

The force of our machine learning models will be that they won't just learn the relationship between one period and a leading indicator, they will also *automatically* understand if there is a relationship between the demand during a specific period and any lagged version of the indicator. For example, we could have an impact on car sales in Q2 if the GDP growth was high in Q1.

Are leading indicator forecasts reliable?

Macro-economic leading indicators

A weakness of adding external information to your model is that you will need to provide your model with a future *prediction* of this indicator. If you want to make a prediction for next year's car sales in Norway, you will have to feed the tool with the GDP growth Norway is going to have next year. But that's already a prediction exercise!

This question of predicting leading indicators is very tricky. Your model will learn the relationship between sales and the leading indicator based on its *actual* historical value. The model might then give a certain importance to the *actual* historical value of this indicator. But is the *predicted* indicator as reliable?

Back in 2007, no-one forecast that the GDP growth of Norway would be 0.4% in 2008 instead of somewhere between 2.6 and 4% (their GDP growth over the previous years).

What would be perfect is to feed the tool each time with GDP as it was *forecast* historically. But this kind of data is rather difficult to obtain (or even impossible), often resulting in the (implicit) assumption that the *forecast* of a leading indicator is as relevant as its *actual* value.
Always be cautious.

Weather

The weather is a typical leading indicator where the prediction accuracy of week+2 is as correct as simply taking the historical average temperature. Let's go back to our ice cream business. If you want to make a prediction of how much you are going to sell in the next 3 days, the temperature might be very relevant. Let's now imagine you need to make an order to a supplier for a special ingredient. The lead time is 1 month. Can you rely on the weather forecast of day +30 to predict your sales? Most likely not.

Depending on the forecast horizon, some leading indicators can be more reliable than others. It is up to you to test different ones based on the data that is available and on their respective prediction accuracy.

Example

Let's try to see if Norway's GDP growth helps our model to forecast the car sales.

Before we discuss the actual accuracy we could obtain by adding the GDP to our forecast model, let's see if we have any relationship between Norway's GDP growth and their car sales.

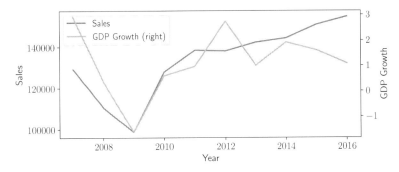

Figure 20.4: Norway's GDP & Car Sales

As you can see on figure 20.4, it seems that there is a correlation between GDP growth and car sales in Norway. Does this mean that our model will benefit from this? That is not guaranteed.

	Training	Test
Regression	17.8	17.8
Tree	16.8	18.1
Forest	13.5	17.5
ETR	9.5	17.3
ETR + GDP	10.9	17.8
AdaBoost	10.7	16.6

Table 20.5: Results with GDP

Unfortunately, as we see on table 20.5, adding the GDP to our ETR model only resulted in a lower accuracy on the test set. Let's see if a feature analysis provides us with some additional insights.

Feature importance

As you can see on figure 20.5, it is clear that GDP is virtually useless for our ETR model to predict car sales. This should be a sufficient clue that we are not adding relevant information to our model but only extra noise. This noise is dangerous as the model can possibly overfit from it (as we saw on table 20.5).

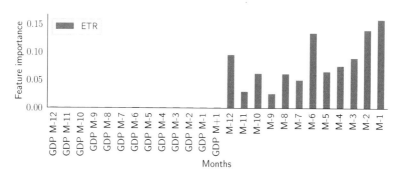

Figure 20.5: GDP importance for car sales

Do It Yourself

Let's imagine that we have an Excel file *GDP.xlsx* that contains the GDP growth of Norway per year[1]. It should look like figure 20.6.

	A	B
1	Year	GDP
2	2006	2,40
3	2007	2,93
4	2008	0,38
5	2009 -	1,62
6	2010	0,60
7	2011	0,97

Figure 20.6: GDP data

---

[1] A simple Google search can get you such data for any country.

Do It Yourself

Let's extract this data from our Excel file back into Python.

```
GDP = pd.read_excel("GDP.xlsx").set_index("Year")
dates = [int(date[:4]) for date in df.columns.values]
X_GDP = [GDP.loc[date,"GDP"] for date in dates]
```

X_GDP is a `NumPy array` that has the same length as our initial historical demand `DataFrame df`.

Now, we have to update our `datasets` function (that we initially made on page 118) so that it can take an exogenous dataset and add it to our X and Y `arrays`. In our function, we will call this exogenous dataset X_exo to be a bit more generalistic than X_GDP.

These are the main changes we will make:

1. We will increase (on lines 5 & 6) our initial X_exo vector into a matrix that has the same size as our historical demand `DataFrame`. In order to do this, we will use the `np.repeat()` function which simply repeats a line over multiple times.
2. When we create the training and test sets, we will concatenate the corresponding exogenous data to each iteration. This is done on lines 12–14 for the training set and on lines 22-24 for the test set.

```
def datasets(df, X_exo, x_len=12, y_len=1, y_test_len=12):

    periods = df.shape[1]
    D = df.values
    X_exo = np.array(X_exo).reshape([1,-1])
    X_exo = np.repeat(X_exo,D.shape[0],axis=0)

    # Training set creation: run through all the possible time windows
    loops = periods + 1 - x_len - y_len - y_test_len
    train = []
    for col in range(loops):
        d = D[:,col:col+x_len+y_len]
        exo = X_exo[:,col:col+x_len+y_len]
        train.append(np.hstack([exo,d]))
    train = np.vstack(train)
    X_train, Y_train = np.split(train,[-y_len],axis=1)

    # Test set creation: unseen "future" data with the demand just before
    max_col_test = periods - x_len - y_len + 1
    test = []
    for col in range(loops,max_col_test):
        d = D[:,col:col+x_len+y_len]
```

```
23            exo = X_exo[:,col:col+x_len+y_len]
24            test.append(np.hstack([exo,d]))
25        test = np.vstack(test)
26        X_test, Y_test = np.split(test,[-y_len],axis=1)
27
28        # this data formatting is needed if we only predict a single period
29        if y_len == 1:
30            Y_train = Y_train.ravel()
31            Y_test = Y_test.ravel()
32
33        return X_train, Y_train, X_test, Y_test
```

From here, you can simply use this function to generate the new train and test arrays. These can then be used in the various models just as before.

Chapter 21

Extreme Gradient Boosting

In 2001, Jerome H. Friedman released his paper "Greedy Function Approximation: A Gradient Boosting Machine"[3], which introduced a new concept to boost trees. His model is called a **Gradient Boosting**. The general concept of Gradient Boosting and Adaptive Boosting is basically the same: stack trees on top of each other based on the model's current mistakes. Only the implementation and the mathematical inner workings differ.

Extreme Gradient Boosting As often, this first algorithm was refined by the original author over time. Later, Tianqi Chen proposed a new gradient boosting algorithm and formalized it in 2016 in his paper "XGBoost: A Scalable Tree Boosting System"[1]. Chen created an efficient implementation of the gradient boosting algorithm (that he called *Extreme Gradient Boosting* or *XGBoost*). His implementation has since then been widely used by the data science community with excellent results. This is simply one of the most powerful machine learning algorithms currently available.

In this chapter, we will focus on XGBoost rather than the *regular* gradient boosting. As said, the difference between AdaBoost, Gradient Boosting and Extreme Gradient Boosting lies in the inner mathematical workings of each model. As users, XGBoost will bring us three improvements compared to AdaBoost & regular Gradient Boosting:

- XGBoost is faster.

- XGBoost is (generally) better.
- XGBoost allows for more parameters to be optimized.

Speed

As you can see on figure 21.1, the implementation of XGBoost is (at least) twice as fast as AdaBoost. Actually, it is more similar to the one needed to train a forest. In contrast, the time to run a regular Gradient Boosting seems to grow exponentially with the maximum depth of the trees. As always, the ETR model is the fastest.

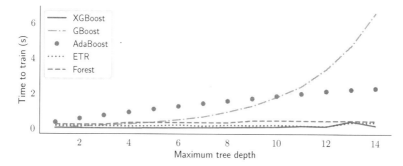

Figure 21.1: Training time for 100 trees

New parameters

XGBoost allows for more tree parameters to be set compared to the implementation of AdaBoost or Gradient Boosting. Let's discuss some of the new interesting parameters.

> **colsample_bylevel** This is the maximum number of features each node inside a tree can make is split on. This means that at each node (i.e. intersection) of each tree, the algorithm will only be able to choose a split on a limited amount of features. These are selected randomly at each node. It is similar to the parameter max_features we used in the other models — except here it is a value per node and not per tree. Typically, this varies between 50% and 90%.
>
> **subsample** This ratio is the % of training samples that each new tree is fitted on. The samples are chosen randomly. This means that

each tree won't be trained on the full training dataset. Typically, this
parameter as well can vary between 50% and 90%.

Both `colsample_bylevel` & `subsample` will restrain the overfitting of
the model. And they will also provide a stronger model by creating more
different trees. Remember that the two ensemble models (forest & ETR)
were also based on the principle that many different predictors can create
a stronger one.

Of course, like for AdaBoost, we can also use `max_depth` & `learning_rate`.

Early stopping

When an XGBoost model is trained on a dataset, we can measure – after
each iteration – its accuracy against an **evaluation** set. If you want to find
the right number of trees for your model, the best practice is of course
to run a random search. But rather than trying different models with a
different number of trees, we could grow our model indefinitely, and stop
it when we do not see any improvement for a number of consecutive
iterations over the evaluation set. When we stop adding new trees (as
they did not bring added value for some time), we will take back the
model as it was at the last iteration that brought extra accuracy to the
evaluation set. With this technique, we get rid of the burden of number-
of-trees optimization and we are sure to grow our model up to the right
level.

As you can see on figures 21.2 & 21.3, the
extra accuracy obtained for each new tree
added to the model decreases over time. After a while, each new tree will slightly *increase*
the error over the evaluation set rather than
decrease it. This is when you want to stop
the model from adding new trees.

```
[15]    validation_0-mae:30.7372
[16]    validation_0-mae:30.6942
[17]    validation_0-mae:30.6457
[18]    validation_0-mae:30.6246
[19]    validation_0-mae:30.5806
[20]    validation_0-mae:30.6182
[21]    validation_0-mae:30.6694
[22]    validation_0-mae:30.6866
[23]    validation_0-mae:30.7165
[24]    validation_0-mae:30.8236
[25]    validation_0-mae:30.864
[26]    validation_0-mae:30.9004
[27]    validation_0-mae:30.9396
[28]    validation_0-mae:30.9402
[29]    validation_0-mae:30.8912
Stopping. Best iteration:
[19]    validation_0-mae:30.5806
```
Figure 21.2: Early stopping in action

This early-stopping technique will help us
avoid overfitting our model to the training
set, and at the same time reduce training time. One stone, two birds. The early-
stopping technique is a very useful capabil-
ity of XGBoost. We will discuss how to do it
yourself on page 192.

There are three parameters that we need to set up for the early stopping
to work properly.

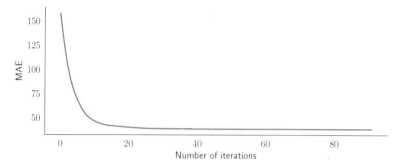

Figure 21.3: Early stopping

eval_set The evaluation set used to evaluate the model after each iteration.

early_stopping_rounds The maximum number of iterations (i.e. new trees) we can do without improving the accuracy on the eval_set.

eval_metric The metric used to evaluate the eval_set. You can use "rmse" for root mean square error[1] or "mae" for mean absolute error.

You can use a subset of the training set as the evaluation set; or the holdout dataset as defined on page 161. What we do not want is to set the test set as the evaluation set. That would be overfitting... Don't do this.

Do It Yourself

Installation

The scikit-learn library proposes an implementation of the original gradient boosting algorithm proposed by J. Friedman. We will actually prefer the library developed around Chen's algorithm[2] to benefit from his efficient and powerful implementation.

If you have a windows machine and use anaconda, you can install it simply by typing in an anaconda console

```
conda install -c anaconda py-xgboost
```

---

[1] Contrary to most of the other scikit-learn models, here we need to pass "rmse" instead of "mse".

[2] You can find it on *xgboost.readthedocs.io*

Do It Yourself

Or, if you have a mac/linux

```
conda install -c conda-forge xgboost
```

First model

The `xgboost` library proposes different functions. You have the *vanilla* ones that are meant to be used independently of any other library. But, in order not to confuse ourselves, we will prefer the functions that were specifically created to work together with `scikit-learn`[1].

Let's start with a simple example.

```
from xgboost.sklearn import XGBRegressor
XGB = XGBRegressor(n_jobs=-1, max_depth=10, n_estimators=100,
    learning_rate=0.2)
XGB = XGB.fit(X_train, Y_train)
```

As you can see, the `xgboost.sklearn` behaves exactly like `scikit-learn`.

You can plot the feature importances in one line thanks to the function `plot_importance` from `xgboost`.

```
import xgboost as xgb
xgb_plot = xgb.plot_importance(XGB)
```

You should obtain a figure like 21.4.

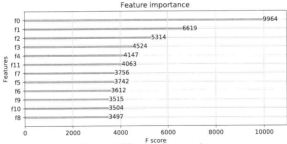

Figure 21.4: XGBoost feature importances

---

[1]You can find the documentation here: xgboost.readthedocs.io/en/latest/python/python_api.html#module-xgboost.sklearn

Early Stopping

If we want to use the early stopping functionality – and we want to use it – we have to pass the parameters `early_stopping_rounds`, `eval_set` and `eval_metric` to the `.fit()` method.

We also have to define an *evaluation* dataset. We can do it by extracting a random part out of the original training set. The function `train_test_split` from `scikit-learn` will do this for us.

```
from sklearn.model_selection import train_test_split
x_train, x_eval, y_train, y_eval = train_test_split(X_train, Y_train, test_size
    =0.15)

from xgboost.sklearn import XGBRegressor
XGB = XGBRegressor(n_jobs=-1, max_depth=10, n_estimators=1000,
    learning_rate=0.2,)
XGB = XGB.fit(x_train, y_train, early_stopping_rounds=10, verbose=True,
    eval_set=[(x_eval,y_eval)], eval_metric="mae" )
```

You can set the parameter `verbose` to `True` to see the results of each iteration (the result is rather impressive). As you now set the `early_stopping_rounds`, you can set the number of estimators (`n_estimators`) to an arbitrarily high number (here 1000).

Parameter optimization

Before we look at how to optimize our XGBoost model thanks to `scikit-learn`, let's define the parameter space we want (`params`) as well as another dictionary with the fitting parameters we want to use (`fit_params`).

```
params = {
    "max_depth": [4,5,6,7,8,10,12],
    "learning_rate": [0.001,0.005,0.01,0.025,0.05,0.1],
    "colsample_bylevel": [0.3,0.4,0.5,0.6,0.7,0.8,0.9],
    "subsample": [0.2,0.3,0.4,0.5,0.6,0.7],
    "n_estimators":[1000]}

fit_params = {
    "early_stopping_rounds":5,
    "eval_set":[(X_holdout,Y_holdout)],
    "eval_metric":"mae",
    "verbose":False}
```

Do It Yourself

We can now use our favorite `scikit-learn` function: `RandomizedSearchCV` to optimize our parameters.

```
from sklearn.model_selection import RandomizedSearchCV

XGB = XGBRegressor()
XGB_cv = RandomizedSearchCV(XGB, params, cv=5, n_jobs=-1, verbose
    =1, n_iter=1000, scoring="neg_mean_absolute_error")
XGB_cv.fit(X_train, Y_train,**fit_params)
```

If you do not remember how `**fit_params` works, you can look at page 156. This is what we obtain:

```
Tuned XGBoost Parameters: {'subsample': 0.3, 'n_estimators': 1000, '
    max_depth': 8, 'learning_rate': 0.01, 'colsample_bylevel': 0.5}
```

Let's run a new model with a full training set (we used a holdout training set for the random search):

```
X_train, Y_train, X_holdout, Y_holdout, X_test, Y_test = datasets(df,holdout
    =0)
x_train, x_eval, y_train, y_eval = train_test_split(X_train, Y_train, test_size
    =0.15)

XGB = XGBRegressor(n_jobs=-1, max_depth=8, n_estimators=1000,
    learning_rate=0.01, subsample=0.3, colsample_bylevel=0.5)
XGB = XGB.fit(x_train, y_train, early_stopping_rounds=10, verbose=False,
    eval_set=[(x_eval,y_eval)], eval_metric="mae")

Y_train_pred = XGB_cv.predict(X_train)
MAE_train = np.mean(abs(Y_train - Y_train_pred))/np.mean(Y_train)
print("XGBoost on training set MAE%:",round(MAE_train*100,1))

Y_test_pred = XGB_cv.predict(X_test)
MAE_test = np.mean(abs(Y_test - Y_test_pred))/np.mean(Y_test)
print("XGBoost on test set MAE%:",round(MAE_test*100,1))
```

This is the accuracy we get now:

```
XGBoost on training set MAE%: 17.8
XGBoost on test set MAE%: 20.5
```

Unfortunately, for our dataset, XGBoost didn't live up to its promise and couldn't deliver a better result than AdaBoost, ETR or our Forest.

	Training	Test
Regression	17.8	17.8
Tree	16.8	18.1
Forest	13.5	17.5
ETR	9.5	17.3
AdaBoost	10.7	16.6
XGBoost	12.3	20.5

Even though XGBoost didn't deliver good results in this example dataset, I can only encourage you **to test it on your own dataset**. It might deliver outstanding results compared to AdaBoost, a forest or ETR.

Multiple periods

Just like AdaBoost, XGBoost unfortunately cannot forecast multiple periods at once. This time we won't be able to use `MultiOutputRegressor` as we did for AdaBoost on page 175, as it cannot deal with the special fitting parameters we need for the early stopping to work.

That's fine, we'll just create two functions to overcome this. The first one — `XGBoost` — will populate an output for one period.

```
def XGBoost(X_train, Y_train, X_test, params):

    from sklearn.model_selection import train_test_split
    x_train, x_eval, y_train, y_eval = train_test_split(X_train, Y_train, test_size=0.15)

    fit_params = {"early_stopping_rounds":5,
        "eval_set":[(x_eval, y_eval)],
        "eval_metric":"mae",
        "verbose":False}

    XGB = XGBRegressor(**params)
    XGB.fit(x_train, y_train, **fit_params)

    return XGB.predict(X_train), XGB.predict(X_test)
```

Pay attention that `fit_params` needs to be declared in the function `XGBoost` as the `eval_set` changes each time.

Do It Yourself

We can now create a second function `XGBoost_multi` that will call `XGBoost` for each period we want to forecast.

```python
def XGBoost_multi(X_train, Y_train, X_test, params):

    Y_train_pred = Y_train.copy()
    Y_test_pred = Y_test.copy()

    for col in range(Y_train.shape[1]):
        results = XGBoost(X_train, Y_train[:,col], X_test, params)
        Y_train_pred[:,col] = results[0]
        Y_test_pred[:,col] = results[1]

    return Y_test_pred, Y_train_pred
```

Chapter 22

Categories

As we saw in chapter 20, we can improve our forecast by enriching our dataset i.e. by bringing external information on top of our historical demand. Note that it is not meaningful for all businesses to bring such external macro-economic elements. On the other hand, every supply chain serves different markets and has different product families. One could think that a machine learning model could benefit from these extra pieces of information: *Am I selling this to market A? Is this product part of family B?*

In our car sales dataset, we could imagine that instead of only having the sales in Norway, we would have the sales in different markets across Europe. You could then feed the algorithm with the sales per country and indicate the market of each data sample (e.g. Sweden, Finland). We could also imagine splitting the different car makers based on price segmentation into 4 different categories: low cost, normal, premium and luxury brands.

Encoding

Unfortunately, most of the current machine learning libraries (including `scikit-learn`) cannot directly deal with categorical inputs. This means that you won't be able to fit your model based on the X_train dataset shown on table 22.1.

The machine learning models we learned can only be trained based on numerical inputs. That means that we will have to transform our categorical inputs into numbers.

	X_train				Y_train
Segment	Demand				Demand
Premium	5	15	10	7	6
Normal	2	3	1	1	1
Low cost	18	25	32	47	56
Luxury	4	1	5	3	2

Table 22.1: X_train with categorical data

Integer encoding

A first way to transform our categories into numbers is simply to allocate a value to each category such as shown on table 22.2.

Weather	Integer
Sunny	1
Cloudy	2
Rainy	3
Snowy	4

Table 22.2: Weather integer encoding

This is a rather simple and straightforward way to transform a categorical input into a numerical one. It is meaningful if you have an **ordinal** relationship between all the categories. An ordinal relationship means that the different categories have a **natural order** between them – even though it might be unclear how one could measure the distance between two categories.

In our example of weather (table 22.2), it makes sense to say that Rainy is higher than Snowy, and Sunny is higher than Rainy. We know this, even though we cannot estimate the distance between Sunny and Rainy. By providing numbers to our machine learning model, the algorithm will be able to *easily* ask questions such as *Is the weather better than* Rainy*?*.

Let's go back to our example of car makers: we could easily imagine classifying them on a scale from 1 (low cost) to 4 (luxury). So that our algorithm would be trained on an X_train dataset that would look like table 22.3.

Limitation In many cases, **the different categories are not naturally ordered**. Providing ordered numbers to the algorithm will confuse it, or make it difficult for it to focus on a couple of specific categories if they were not allocated to consecutive numbers. If you do not have naturally

Encoding

Segment	X_train Demand				Y_train Demand
3	5	15	10	7	6
2	2	3	1	1	1
1	18	25	32	47	56
4	4	1	5	3	2

Table 22.3: X_train with integer encoding

ordered categories, you'll have to find another way to feed them to your model.

One-hot label encoding

If we do not have naturally ordered categories (such as different markets or product families), we'll use a technique called **one-hot encoding**[1]. Let's explain this with an example. Imagine we have a dataset with 4 different markets: Europe, USA, China & India. To encode this categorical information into numbers, we'll create one boolean[2] column per country such as shown on table 22.4.

Market	Europe	USA	China	India
Europe	1	0	0	0
USA	0	1	0	0
China	0	0	1	0
India	0	0	0	1

Table 22.4: One-hot encoding

This technique is called one-hot encoding as each line will only have one element different from zero, or only one hot value.

				X_train				Y_train
	Segment			Demand				Demand
0	0	1	0	5	15	10	7	6
0	1	0	0	2	3	1	1	1
1	0	0	0	18	25	32	47	56
0	0	0	1	4	1	5	3	2

Table 22.5: X_train with one-hot encoding

---

[1] Otherwise known as dummification
[2] A boolean is a value that is either True or False: 1 or 0.

One-hot encoding is rather helpful for an algorithm to quickly identify one category (or to exclude one). Our tree-based models can easily ask a question such as "Is Europe > 0?" that is to say that the market is Europe and not USA, China or India. The algorithm can also easily exclude one market if needed by asking the question "Is Europe < 1?".

This wouldn't be possible with the integer-encoding technique. If markets were encoded as consecutive numbers, you would need to ask at least two questions to exclude or include only one market. This is simply less efficient than with the one-hot technique.

One less column? Actually, when you look at table 22.4, you could get the same information with one column less. One could say that Market is Europe if Market isn't USA, China or India.

Market	USA	China	India
Europe	0	0	0
USA	1	0	0
China	0	1	0
India	0	0	1

Table 22.6: One-hot encoding (with one less column)

This technique is used by some to reduce the number of columns in our dataset while keeping the same amount of information. Sure. But, now, if our algorithm needs to exclude Europe, it will need to ask 3 questions (*Is USA < 1? Is China < 1?* and finally *Is India < 1?*). This is of course not efficient. To have one column less in our dataset might not be worth this loss of efficiency.

Do It Yourself

Data preparation

As a dummy example, we will categorize our car makers between Normal and Luxury brands. We will do this easily by first defining a list of luxury brands

```
luxury_brands = ["Aston Martin"," Bentley"," Ferrari"," Jaguar"," Lamborghini
    "," Lexus"," Lotus"," Maserati"," McLaren"," Porsche"," Tesla"]
```

Do It Yourself

We can now define a new column Segment in our dataset. To do this, we will iterate through df.index and check for each index if it is in Luxury.

```
df["Segment"] = [brand in luxury_brands for brand in df.index]
```

We will now replace the values in df.Segment by either Normal or Luxury to properly format it.

```
df.Segment.replace({True:"Luxury",False:"Normal"},inplace=True)
```

You should obtain the same result as on figure 22.1.

```
Period       2007-01  2007-02  2007-03  ...  2016-12  2017-01  Luxury
Make                                     ...
Alfa Romeo        16        9       21  ...        3        6   False
Aston Martin       0        0        1  ...        0        0    True
Audi             599      498      682  ...      827      565   False
BMW              352      335      365  ...      866     1540   False
Bentley            0        0        0  ...        0        0    True
```
Figure 22.1: Historical dataset

One-hot label encoding

We will use the pandas function get_dummies() to encode the Luxury column as one-hot vectors. This function takes a couple of parameters:

columns (list, default = None)
By default, get_dummies() will transform into one-hot vectors all the columns that are defined as either categories[1] or objects (e.g. strings). You can also specify a list of columns you want to encode as one-hot vectors.

prefix (string or list of strings, default = None)
By default, pandas will give the initial column name to all the new one-hot columns, but you can input a new name via this parameter.

prefix_sep (string or list of strings, default = "_")
get_dummies() will append the value of the category to each new one-hot column name. In our example, we will get two columns: Luxury_True and Luxury_False.

drop_first (bool, default = False)
This boolean will determine if get_dummies() will get rid of the first one-hot column (as discussed on page 200).

---
[1]A specific data type that pandas can use. Feel free to check www.supchains.com/article/pandas-categories/ for more information.

Thanks to get_dummies(), we can format our dataset in just one line.

```
1  df = pd.get_dummies(df,columns=["Segment"],prefix_sep='_')
```

You should now have something similar to figure 22.2

	2007-01	2007-02	...	Luxury_False	Luxury_True
Make			...		
Alfa Romeo	16	9	...	1	0
Aston Martin	0	0	...	0	1
Audi	599	498	...	1	0
BMW	352	335	...	1	0
Bentley	0	0	...	0	1

Figure 22.2: Historical dataset with one-hot columns

Dataset creation

Now that we have properly formatted our DataFrame df, we can create our datasets X_train, Y_train, X_test and Y_test. In order to do so, we will update our datasets function (that we initially made on page 118) so that it can properly use a categorical input.

The idea is that we will flag the categorical columns in the historical dataset df based on their names. Remember that we gave all our categorical columns a specific prefix_sep, so that they all contain "_" in their name (or any other string you want).

These are then the new steps we will do take our function:

line 1 Use a new parameter sep that will contain the character (or string) to identify the categorical columns.

line 3 Define col_cat as a list of booleans that will flag df columns (based on sep) as being either historical sales or categorical information.

line 4 Define D as the historical sales (as before) by excluding the categorical columns from df.

line 6 Define C as the categorical columns.

lines 14&22 Stack C to both X_train & X_test. We'll first have to prepare C by stacking it on top of itself multiple times to match the shape of both X_train and X_test.

```
1  def datasets(df, x_len=12, y_len=1, y_test_len=12, sep="_"):
2
3      col_cat = [col for col in df.columns if sep in col]
```

Do It Yourself

```
 4     D = df.drop(col_cat,axis=1).values
 5     periods = D.shape[1]
 6     C = df[col_cat].values
 7
 8     loops = periods + 1 - x_len - y_len - y_test_len
 9     train = []
10     for col in range(loops):
11         train.append(D[:,col:col+x_len+y_len])
12     train = np.vstack(train)
13     X_train, Y_train = np.split(train,[x_len],axis=1)
14     X_train = np.hstack((np.vstack([C]*loops),X_train))
15
16     max_col_test = periods - x_len - y_len + 1
17     test = []
18     for col in range(loops,max_col_test):
19         test.append(D[:,col:col+x_len+y_len])
20     test = np.vstack(test)
21     X_test, Y_test = np.split(test,[x_len],axis=1)
22     X_test = np.hstack((np.vstack([C]*(max_col_test-loops)),X_test))
23
24     # this data formatting is needed if we only predict a single period
25     if y_len == 1:
26         Y_train = Y_train.ravel()
27         Y_test = Y_test.ravel()
28
29     return X_train, Y_train, X_test, Y_test
```

Integer encoding

Let's use another technique to transform our `df.Segment` column into a readable format for our models. We will now transform it into integers. In order to do this, we will use the `.replace()` method on our `DataFrame`.

```
df.Segment.replace({"Normal":1,"Luxury":2},inplace=True)
```

```
Period         2007-01  2007-02  2007-03  ...  2016-12  2017-01  Segment
Make                                      ...
Alfa Romeo          16        9       21  ...        3        6        1
Aston Martin         0        0        1  ...        0        0        2
Audi               599      498      682  ...      827      565        1
BMW                352      335      365  ...      866     1540        1
Bentley              0        0        0  ...        0        0        2
```

Figure 22.3: Historical dataset with integer encoding

From here, we can simply use the Datasets function we just defined on page 202 by passing "Segment" to its parameter sep.

```
X_train, Y_train, X_test, Y_test = datasets(df, x_len=12, y_len=1, y_test_len
    =12, sep="Segment")
```

Chapter 23

Clustering

As discussed in chapter 22, it can be helpful for both the data scientists and the models to classify the various products they have. Unfortunately, you do not always receive a pre-classified dataset. Could a machine learning model help us classify it? Yes, of course.

Supervised learning   All the machine learning models we have seen so far are called **supervised** models. This means that you feed the algorithm both an input and an output – as we saw in chapter 12 – and it is up to the algorithm to understand the relationship(s) between these inputs and outputs. Of course, you cannot ask your algorithm to make a forecast if you never show it what a good forecast looks like.

Unsupervised learning   Another type of algorithm allows the machine to identify relationships in the data *without* a specified output. It means that the algorithm will somehow order (categorize) the different data observations itself. This is called **unsupervised** learning. You can simply see it as asking your algorithm to give a label to each data observation.

Unsupervised learning can cluster anything from products to clients or from social behaviours to neighbourhoods in a city.

K-means

A very famous unsupervised machine learning model is called **K-means**. This algorithm will classify each data observation into k different clusters. Let's look in detail how this works.

K-means algorithm
1. Randomly define **k centers**.
2. Associate each data observation with its closest center. We call a **cluster** all the area that is related to a center.
3. Update each cluster center by moving it to the middle of all the data observations associated to it (i.e. all the data observations within its cluster).
4. Repeat steps 2 & 3 until the cluster centers do not move anymore.

Note that even though this algorithm might look very linear and logical, **the results are actually random**. This is due to the initialization of the algorithm. Depending on the different initial *random* center positions, the final clusters might differ.

Distance

When you ask a K-means model to organize your dataset, you need to give it a mathematical definition of the *distance* between two data samples. One could think that there only exists one definition of the distance between two points, but mathematicians actually came up with many different ones.

Let's keep it simple for our example and define the distance between two points as the Euclidean[1] distance. The Euclidean distance is basically the technical term to define the distance as we use it in our day-to-day lives: simply the length of a straight line between two points.

Let's define the **inertia** of a K-means model as the sum of the distances between each point and its associated center. The lower the inertia, the more "accurate" the model. Reducing the inertia of such a model is very easy: just add more clusters! As you can see on figure 23.1, the more, the better.

Actually, more clusters might result in a lower inertia (i.e. more compact clusters), but these clusters might also get less meaningful and – as we saw in chapter 22 – come with a higher risk of overfitting.

---
[1] Euclid was a Greek geometrician around 300 BC

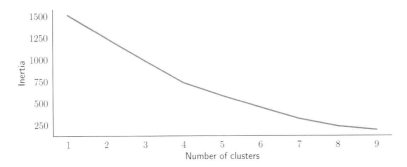

Figure 23.1: Number of clusters

Looking for meaningful centers

We just learned a very powerful & automated way to label an entire dataset thanks to machine learning. But how can we apply this to our historical demand?

The question you should ask yourself is: *what are the features I want my products to be categorized on?* Depending on each dataset, you might prefer different approaches. Here are some ideas:

Volume We can obviously start categorizing products based on their sales volume. Most likely, this categorization won't provide so much added value, as you could just do a good old Pareto classification[1] to get a similar result.

Additive seasonality If we cluster the products based on their additive seasonality factors (as defined in chapter 11), we will cluster them based on their average volume **and** their seasonality. You might then end up with groups containing just a few products.

Multiplicative seasonality If we take the multiplicative seasonal factors (as defined in chapter 9), our products will then be categorized only based on their seasonal behaviour – irrespective of their absolute size. This sounds much better.

As for most of our models, you will have to try different techniques (and different numbers of clusters) until you find the one that is right for your business.

---

[1] A Pareto classification is a thumb rule to divide a dataset into 3 classes (ABC) based on volume. A class is composed of the products that account for 80% of the total demand, B for the next top 15% and C gets the remaining small ones.

Clustering on seasonal factors

A very interesting way to visualize seasonal clusters is to plot a heatmap (we'll see on page 212 how to make one). This kind of visualization will help you *see* the seasonal factors of each cluster. We plotted one on figure 23.2 where we see the cluster centers of dummy products based on their multiplicative seasonal factors (as defined in chapter 9).

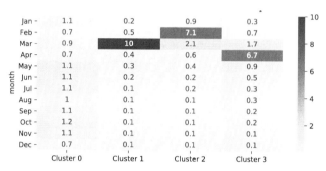

Figure 23.2: Cluster visualization

This heatmap might look strange to you. It seems that cluster 0 contains flat products: see how the seasonal factors are close to 1 (or 100% if you interpret them as percentages). We also have three clusters with extreme seasonalities (clusters 1–3). It seems that the products in these clusters are (more or less) only sold one month per year.

This very strange behaviour is due to the fact that we have a few products that we sold only in March or February, so that their seasonal factors will look like: $[0, 0, 12, 0, 0, 0, 0, 0, 0, 0, 0, 0]$[1]. Our K-means algorithm deals with these extreme values by creating some very specific clusters just for them. Basically, these extreme seasonal factors are **so extreme** that they are not like any other seasonal factors and will require a cluster just for them as their (Euclidean) distance to any other seasonal factors is too long.

Due to this, the clusters we have are not meaningful, let's see how we can tackle this.

---

[1] Remember that the sum of the multiplicative seasonal factors should be 12 (as there are 12 periods). You can observe it on figure 23.2, where the sum of each cluster's seasonal factors is 12. Don't hesitate to check page 73 for more information.

Looking for meaningful centers

Scaling

The K-means algorithm is very sensitive to extreme values (that, by definition, are far away from any other values), so that we will have to normalize all the seasonal factors. It means that the seasonal factors of each product will be reduced in order to have a mean of 0 and a range[1] of 1. In order to do so, we have to divide each set of seasonal factors by its range and then subtract its mean. This will flatten the extreme cases and should allow the K-means algorithm to give more meaningful clusters.

If we perform a clustering on our new scaled seasonal factors, we obtain a meaningful result as shown on figure 23.3.

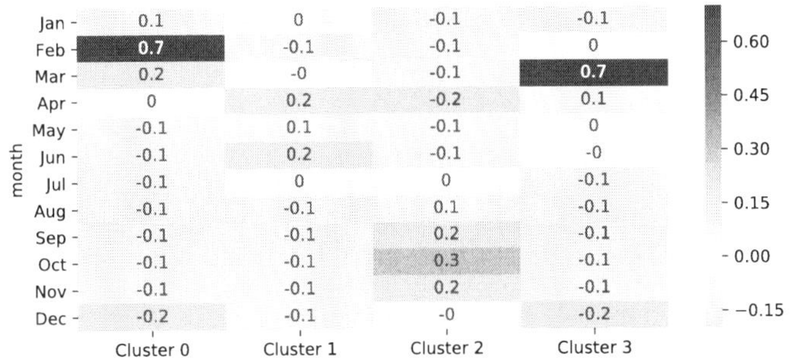

Figure 23.3: Scaled clusters

We now clearly see proper cluster centers that make sense to us. See how Clusters 0 & 3 show products that we sell in February and March (respectively), whereas Cluster 1 contains flatter products with a modest high season in April/June. Finally, Cluster 2 contains the products that have a high season around October.

Recap

K-means is very sensitive to scaling; always remember to scale your dataset before applying this technique. As we did here, it is always a best practice to visualize your results to check that they are meaningful. Another good check is to count the number of products in each cluster: if you obtain some clusters with only a few items, that might be a clue that the clusters are not meaningful.

---

[1] range = maximum - minimum

Do It Yourself

Seasonal Factors

Let's first compute the (multiplicative) seasonal factors. In order to do so, we will create a function **seasonal_factors** that will return the seasonal factors based on a historical demand dataset.

```
def seasonal_factors(df):
    s = pd.DataFrame(index=df.index)
    for month in range(12):
        col = [x for x in range(df.shape[1]) if x%12==month] # Column
            indices that match this month
        s[month+1] = np.mean(df.iloc[:,col],axis=1) # Compute season
            average for this month
    s = s.divide(s.mean(axis=1),axis=0)
    return s
```

We will now create a **scaler** function that will return the seasonality factors scaled with a range of 1 and a mean of 0.

```
def scaler(s):
    mean = s.mean(axis=1)
    maxi = s.max(axis=1)
    mini = s.min(axis=1)
    s = s.subtract(mean,axis=0)
    s = s.divide(maxi-mini,axis=0).fillna(0)
    return s
```

Cluster definition

Let's now use the k-means algorithm to identify the different clusters among our products (we assume **df** to contain the historical demand per product).

```
import numpy as np
import pandas as pd
from sklearn.cluster import KMeans

s = seasonal_factors(df)
s = scaler(s)

kmeans = KMeans(n_clusters=n, random_state=0).fit(s_normalize)
df["Group"] = kmeans.predict(s_normalize) #Add the results back into df
```

Do It Yourself

The KMeans model from scikit-learn takes as an input the number of clusters we want (n_clusters) and can take a random_state as well.

> random_state assures that the results are reproducible by forcing scikit-learn to always use the same random values (if any).

Giving a specific random_state to KMeans is rather helpful as we can expect the same clusters each time we call the algorithm. This will make our analyst life much easier (you can actually give a random_state to most of scikit-learn models).

Experimentation

There is definitely no silver bullet when it comes determining how many clusters you need to define. In order to do so, you can rely on three main tools:

- plotting the inertia vs the number of clusters;
- visualizing the seasonal factors;
- analyzing the number of products by cluster.

Let's discuss these in details.

Inertia

Let's loop through different numbers of clusters and plot the inertia obtained for each of these.

```
from sklearn.cluster import KMeans

# define the dataframe that will contain our results
results = pd.DataFrame(columns=["Inertia","Number of clusters"])

for n in range(1,10):
    kmeans = KMeans(n_clusters=n, random_state=0).fit(s_normalize)
    results = results.append({"Inertia":kmeans.inertia_,"Number of clusters"
        :n},ignore_index=True)

# plot the results
results.set_index("Number of clusters").plot()
```

This code will plot a figure similar to figure 23.1 on page 207.

Cluster visualization

In order to plot a heatmap similar to figure 23.3 on page 209, we will use a new library: seaborn.

Seaborn is a Python library that aims to create advanced statistical graphs. As you will see below, it is actually very simple to use. seaborn was published in 2012 by Michael Waskom. The official documentation is available on seaborn.pydata.org, and like the one for pandas, NumPy or scikit-learn, it is very easy to read. Don't hesitate to look for inspiration on seaborn.pydata.org/examples.

The convention is to import seaborn as sns[1].

```
centers = kmeans.cluster_centers_
centers = pd.DataFrame(centers,columns=range(1,13)).transpose()

# Cleaning & formatting
import calendar
month_names = [calendar.month_abbr[month_idx] for month_idx in range(1,
    13)]
column_names = ["Cluster "+str(x) for x in range(centers.shape[1])]
centers.index = month_names
centers.columns = column_names

import seaborn as sns
sns.heatmap(centers, annot=True,center=0,cmap="RdBu_r")
```

When you call sns.heatmap, you can choose the color map you want thanks to the parameter cmap. In the example above, we use a color map going from blue to red by passing cmap="RdBu_r". The parameter center will define where the color map will be centered.

Number of products per cluster

We can also count the number of products inside each cluster to understand if these are meaningful. This can be done in one line of code.

```
print(df["Group"].value_counts().sort_index())
```

---

[1] sns was intended as a joke by the author Michael Waskom who choose these based on the initials of a TV-show character.

Do It Yourself

If some clusters contain a low amount of products, it means that either you have too many clusters for them to be relevant, or you should look at another set of (scaled?) features to classify your products.

XGBoost – 2016
//

pandas – 2008

Extremely Random Trees – 2006
//

NumPy – 2005

GBoost – 2001
//

AdaBoost – 1997
//
Forest – 1995
//

Python – 1991

Damped trends – 1985
● ● ● ● ● ● ● ● ● ● ● ●

Machine Learning
//
Python

Exponential Smoothing
● ● ● ● ● ● ● ● ● ● ● ●

Tree – 1963
//

Winters – 1960
● ● ● ● ● ● ● ● ● ● ● ●

Holt – 1957
● ● ● ● ● ● ● ● ● ● ● ●

Now it's your turn!

The real purpose of this book was actually not to explain different models. It was to **give you the appetite to use them**. This book is a toolbox that gave you the tools & models to create your own forecast. Hopefully, it has also ignited ideas for you to create *unique* models and the methodology to test them.

We have learned in part I how to create a powerful statistical baseline forecast thanks to the different exponential smoothing models. Moreover, we have discussed different ideas (especially the different initialization methods) to tweak them to any dataset. We have also created a very robust model to detect (and correct!) outliers in an automated fashion. We have discussed different forecast KPIs to make sure that you will be able to properly assess your models.

In the second part of the book, we have discovered how machine learning could create advanced forecast models that could learn relationships across a whole dataset. Machine learning will allow you to classify your products and to uncover any potential *complex* relationship with internal or external factors.

The most important message is: **You can do it**.

First focus on the most important parts of your model. Then grow repeatedly by adding (and testing!) new layers. Avoid overfitting. Avoid the temptation to add too much complexity at once. Openly discuss your ideas, models and results with others. To finally achieve astonishing results.

Acknowledgements

Discussing problems, models and potential solutions has always been my one of my favorite ways to find new ideas. And test them. As for any other big project, when I started to write *Data Science for Supply Chain Forecast*, I knew discussions with various people would be needed in order to receive feedback. Thankfully, I have always been able to count on many friends, mentors and experts to share and exchange upon these thoughts.

First and foremost, I want to express my thanks to professor Alassane Ndiaye who has been a true source of inspiration for me ever since we have met in 2011. Not only does Alassane have the ability to maintain the big picture and stay on course in any situation – especially when it is comes to supply chain – but he also has a sense of leadership that encourages each and every one to shine and come face to face with their true potential. Thank you for your trust, your advice and for inspiring me Alassane.

Furthermore, I would like to thank Henri-Xavier Benoist and Jon San Andres from Bridgestone for their support, their confidence and the many opportunities that they have given me. Together, we have achieved many fruitful endeavors, knowing that many more are to come in the future.

Of course, I also need to mention Lokad's team for their support, vision and their incredible ability to create edge models. Special thanks to Johannes Vermorel (CEO & founder) for his support and inspiration he is a real visionary for quantitative supply chain models. I would also like to thank the all-star team composed of Simon Schalit, Alexandre Magny as well as Rafael de Rezende for the incredible inventory model we have created together for Bridgestone.

There are few passionate professionals in the field of supply chains who can both deal with the business reality as well as with the advanced quantitative models. Professor Bram De Smet is one of those, who has inspired me – and many other supply chain professionals around the globe for years. In February 2018, when we finally got the chance to meet in person, I shared my idea of writing a book about supply chain and data science. He simply said "Just go for it and enjoy it the fullest". Thank you, Bram for believing in me and pushing me to take that first step.

Just like forests are stronger than a single tree by itself, I like to surround myself with supportive and bright friends. I especially would like to thank each and every one of the following amazing people for their feedback & support: Gil Vander Marcken, Charles Hoffremont, Bruno Deremince & Emmeline Everaert, Romain Faurès, Alexis Nsamzinshuti, Franois Grisay, Fabio Periera, Nicolas Pary & Flore Dargent, Gilles Belleflamme. And of course, a special thanks goes to Camille Pichot. They have all helped me to make this book more comprehensive and more complete. I have always appreciated feedback from others to improve my work, and I would never have been able to write this book alone without the help of this fine team of supportive friends.

On another note, I would also like to mention Daniel Stanton for the time he took to share his experience about business book publishing with me.

Last, but not least, I would like to truly thank Jonathan Vardakis. Without his dedicated reviews and corrections, this book would simply not have come to its full completion. Throughout this collaboration, I have realized that we are perfect fit together to write a book. Many thanks to you Jon.

Nicolas Vandeput
nicolas.vandeput@supchains.com

Bibliography

[1] Tianqi Chen and Carlos Guestrin. "XGBoost: A Scalable Tree Boosting System". In: *Proceedings of the 22nd ACM SIGKDD International Conference on Knowledge Discovery and Data Mining*. KDD '16. San Francisco, California, USA: ACM, 2016, pp. 785–794. ISBN: 978-1-4503-4232-2. URL: http://doi.acm.org/10.1145/2939672.2939785.

[2] Yoav Freund and Robert E Schapire. "A Decision-Theoretic Generalization of On-Line Learning and an Application to Boosting". In: *Journal of Computer and System Sciences* 55.1 (1997), pp. 119–139. ISSN: 0022-0000. DOI: https://doi.org/10.1006/jcss.1997.1504.

[3] Jerome H. Friedman. "Greedy Function Approximation: A Gradient Boosting Machine". In: *The Annals of Statistics* 29.5 (2001), pp. 1189–1232. ISSN: 00905364. URL: http://www.jstor.org/stable/2699986.

[4] Everette S. Gardner and Ed. Mckenzie. "Forecasting Trends in Time Series". In: *Management Science* 31.10 (1985), pp. 1237–1246. DOI: 10.1287/mnsc.31.10.1237. eprint: https://doi.org/10.1287/mnsc.31.10.1237. URL: https://doi.org/10.1287/mnsc.31.10.1237.

[5] Pierre Geurts, Damien Ernst, and Louis Wehenkel. "Extremely randomized trees". In: *Machine Learning* 63.1 (Apr. 2006), pp. 3–42. URL: https://doi.org/10.1007/s10994-006-6226-1.

[6] Tin Kam Ho. "Random Decision Forests". In: ICDAR '95 (1995), pp. 278–. URL: http://dl.acm.org/citation.cfm?id=844379.844681.

[7] Charles C. Holt. "Forecasting seasonals and trends by exponentially weighted moving averages". In: *International Journal of Forecasting*

20.1 (2004), pp. 5–10. URL: https://doi.org/10.1016/j.ijforecast.2003.09.015.

[8] MITx. *Introduction to Computer Science and Programming Using Python.* URL: www.edx.org/course/introduction-to-computer-science-and-programming-using-python.

[9] James Morgan and John A. Sonquist. "Problems in the Analysis of Survey Data and a Proposal". In: *Journal of the American Statistical Association* 58 (June 1963), pp. 415–434.

[10] Dan Gardner Philip E. Tetlock. *Superforecasting: The Art and Science of Prediction.* Broadway Books, 2016.

[11] George Athanasopoulos Rob J Hyndman. *Forecasting: principles and practice.* 2018.

[12] Nate Silver. *The Signal and the Noise: Why So Many Predictions Fail–but Some Don't.* Penguin Books, 2015.

[13] Peter R. Winters. "Forecasting Sales by Exponentially Weighted Moving Averages". In: *Management Science* 6.3 (1960), pp. 324–342. URL: https://doi.org/10.1287/mnsc.6.3.324.

Glossary

alpha
  Smoothing factor applied to the demand level in the various exponential smoothing models. In theory: $0 < \alpha \leq 1$, in practice: $0 < \alpha \leq 0.5$. *See page* 28

array
  Data structure defined in NumPy. It is a list or a matrix of numeric values. *See page* 7

beta
  Smoothing factor applied to the trend in the various exponential smoothing models. In theory: $0 < \beta \leq 1$, in practice: $0 < \beta \leq 0.5$. *See page* 41

bullwhip effect
  The bullwhip effect is observed in supply chains where small variations in the downstream demand result in massive variations in the upstream supply chain. *See page* 45

data leakage
  In the case of forecast models, describes a situation where a model is given pieces of information about the future demand. *See page* 30

DataFrame
  Table of data as defined by the pandas library. It is similar to a table in Excel or an SQL database. *See page* 9

demand observation
  This is the demand of a product during one period. For example, a demand observation could be the demand of a product in January last year. *See page* 4

gamma
　　Smoothing factor applied to the seasonality (either additive or multiplicative) in the triple exponential smoothing models. In theory: $0 < \gamma \leq 1$, in practice: $0.05 < \gamma \leq 0.3$. *See page* 71

holdout dataset
　　Defined subset of the training set that is kept aside to validate a model. Most often, the holdout set is made of the last periods of the training set in order to replicate a test set. *See page* 161

Mean Absolute Error
　　$MAE = \frac{1}{n}\sum |e_t|$ *See page* 17

Mean Absolute Percentage Error
　　$MAPE = \frac{1}{n}\sum \frac{|e_t|}{d_t}$ *See page* 17

Mean Square Error
　　$MSE = \frac{1}{n}\sum e_t^2$ *See page* 18

naïve forecast
　　This is the simplest forecast model: the future forecast is the very last observation. *See page* 4

noise
　　In statistics, the noise is an unexplained variation in the data. It is often due to the randomness of the different processes at hand. *See page* 5

NumPy
　　One of the most famous Python libraries. It is focused on numeric computation. The basic data structure in NumPy is an array. *See page* 7

pandas
　　Python library specialized in data formatting and manipulation. Allows the use of DataFrames to store data in tables. *See page* 9

phi
　　Damping factor applied to the trend in the exponential smoothing models. This reduces the trend after each period. In theory: $0 < \phi \leq 1$, in practice: $0.7 \leq \phi \leq 1$. *See page* 61

Root Mean Square Error
　　$RMSE = \sqrt{\frac{1}{n}\sum e_t^2}$ *See page* 18

test dataset
　　Dataset we keep aside in order to test our algorithm against unseen data after its fitting/training. *See page* 37

Glossary

training dataset
Dataset we use to fit (or train) our algorithm. *See page* 37

validation dataset
Random subset of the training set that is kept aside to validate a model. *See page* 129

Printed in Poland
by Amazon Fulfillment
Poland Sp. z o.o., Wrocław